D0065142

The Long View

Reflections on Life, God, and Nature

notes from 7 siete ranch

Don Underwood

Abingdon Press
Nashville

The Long View: Reflections on Life, God, and Nature

Copyright © 2013 by Donald W. Underwood

Library of Congress Cataloging-in-Publication Data

Underwood, Don, 1948-
  The long view : reflections on life, God, and nature / Don Underwood.
    pages   cm
  ISBN 978-1-4267-7597-0 (book / hardback / with printed dust jacket casebound : alk. paper)
1. Meditations. I. Title.
  BV4832.3.U53 2013
  242—dc23
                                                              2013020219

Scripture quotations marked NRSV are taken from the New Revised Standard Version of the Bible, copyright 1989, Division of Christian Education of the National Council of the Churches of Christ in the United States of America. Used by permission. All rights reserved.

Scripture quotations marked NIV are taken from the Holy Bible, New International Version®, NIV®. Copyright © 1973, 1978, 1984, 2011 by Biblica, Inc.™ Used by permission of Zondervan. All rights reserved worldwide. www.zondervan.com. The "NIV" and "New International Version" are trademarks registered in the United States Patent and Trademark Office by Biblica, Inc.™

Scripture quotations noted CEB are from The Common English Bible. Copyright © 2011 by Common English Bible. All rights reserved. Used by permission.www.commonenglishbible.com.

Scripture quotations marked KJV are from The Authorized (King James) Version. Rights in the Authorized Version in the United Kingdom are vested in the Crown. Reproduced by permission of the Crown's patentee, Cambridge University Press.

13 14 15 16 17 18 19 20 21 22—10 9 8 7 6 5 4 3 2 1
MANUFACTURED IN THE UNITED STATES OF AMERICA

Acknowledgments

Every once in a while I will actually read the acknowledgments section of a book. I assume it is out of pure curiosity, or maybe an attempt to peek into the private life of one whose writing I have appreciated. But I have never fully understood the reason for this little section until recently.

Now I understand completely. Writing and publishing a book is an enormous project that cannot be accomplished by one person. My own experience with this has led me to consider the thought that this section should be at the beginning of the book, in bold letters, rather than at the end. I'm quite sure that anyone who has ever published a book would agree with me.

So here goes, and with such utter gratitude for those whom I will name and for those who will inevitably be left out but whose encouragement through the years has meant so much. I trust you know who you are.

Without Dr. Walt Purkey, friend and colleague, this book would have never been published. For years he has urged me to write it, and he finally just took it on as a personal mission. His commitment to sharing the message—including philosophy and theology—led him to collate and categorize hundreds of columns. He then guided me through the process of putting it together, and refused to allow me to put it off "one more year." He recruited church members Ron Kolb, Kay Norris, and Rita Ward to rank and select the columns for the original draft. Rita

Ward also proofread and suggested ideas for the introductions to the chapters. I am ever grateful to them all.

My good friend Patsy Morriss did the editing on the first drafts. I had insisted that she be paid, and she had agreed. But when asked for her bill, she said simply, "Just send me an autographed copy." Patsy, the first one goes to you.

No one could be more blessed than I when it comes to staff. Brilliant and hard charging, they have supported this project in multiple ways, often citing their belief in the message and the need to communicate it to a wider audience. They have advised, proofread, encouraged. They have put up with me. Many of them have become highly valued friends and confidants who have been really important traveling companions in both good and tough times. Mary Harris, my friend for thirty years, deserves a special word here. Other than immediate family, she knows me better than anyone, and, inexplicably, she continues to smile while in my presence. Also, my thanks to Charlotte Popelarski, my assistant for well over two decades. She has published the columns in our church newsletter every week during that time, serving occasionally as impromptu editor.

The Reverend Jan Davis has been both friend extraordinaire and wise colleague. She has played a role in most of the major projects I've been involved in for the last fifteen years, and she deserves credit for much of the success we have enjoyed. She suggested the name for Siete Ranch, and for years she has said, "Write the book." As always, I am now saluting and reporting, "Mission accomplished."

Laura B. Nichol, my friend and sometimes coach, played a major role as both encourager and mentor, to both me and our staff, in getting this book off the ground. She dropped into my life anonymously one day on a conference call, and over the period of a year we became great friends before ever meeting face to face. Was that luck or was that God? I think it was God.

It may be unusual to name the president of the publishing house in this section, but Neil Alexander is much more than that to me. Ours is an unusual friendship forged in the fires that spring up when pursuing change in the life of the church. No one can turn a phrase better than Neil, so I won't even attempt it in my description of him. He is, quite simply, courageous, wise, and loyal.

Pamela Clements guided the publication at Abingdon with a remarkable combination of passion and professionalism, and in the process we became friends. She and her editors, particularly Alton Gansky, taught me much about both the art and the business of publishing a book, and I will always be grateful.

There are two groups of people who deserve my most heartfelt thanks. The first is composed of the members of Christ United Methodist Church in Plano. They have inspired many of the columns, have been faithful readers, and have responded through the years with requests for a book. Without them, we would not be here. Second, the members of my family, living both in this life and the next, have been my greatest inspiration. I had grandparents who left indelible footprints on both my heart and mind, and parents who raised me with love and wisdom. My wife, Bobby, and sons, Adam and Joshua, have both tolerated and encouraged me for over three decades. And then, of course, my grandchildren. The next generation. The reason we should always take the long view.

For Liam and Benjamin

Contents

INTRODUCTION / xi

ABOUT THE SIETE BRAND / xv

1. THE JOURNEY / 1

The Road, Part 1 / 2

The Road, Part 2 / 3

Confession / 5

Pray / 7

The Café / 8

Dreams / 9

The Railroad Truck / 10

Fog / 12

2. INSPIRING LIVES / 15

Sacrifice / 16

Hats / 18

Big Spur / 19

John Bengel / 20

One Last Call / 21

Bonham / 23

A Father's Sacrifice / 25

Johnny / 27

A Dog Story / 28

Miracle on the Hudson / 30

Chasing the Big Bucks! / 31

Contents

Family Reunion / 33

Saragosa / 34

Mama / 36

3. MEMORIES / 39

The Good Old Days / 39

The Old Icehouse / 41

Junk Folder / 43

The Reunion / 44

1948 Studebaker / 46

Blessing Us in Disguise / 47

The First Time / 48

The Laundry / 49

The Legacy / 51

School / 52

Mothers / 54

Disconnecting / 55

"No Noise on My Fingers" / 57

In the Company of Men / 58

4. NATURE / 61

Serenity / 62

The Mesquite Tree / 63

Simple Faith / 64

The Mustard Seed / 65

Hot! / 67

Well Water / 68

The Wheat Harvest / 70

Cold Front / 71

Rain / 73

BlackBerry Heaven / 75

Disastrous Christmas / 76

Don't Miss the Diversions / 77

The Gashouse Gang / 79

Coat Hangers / 80

Contents

Small Things Make a Difference / 81

And the Lights Went Out / 83

Grand Canyon / 84

A Really Big God / 86

5. ALL GOD'S CREATURES / 89

The Dance / 90

Puppy / 91

A Promise Kept / 92

Spur Tracks / 94

RH2 / 95

Save Us a Place / 96

Horses / 97

Deer Tracks in the Arena / 99

Mama Cows / 100

Horse Language / 102

6. PRIORITIES / 105

Things / 106

Sitting / 107

Stop! / 109

Thoughts from Siete Ranch / 110

Slow Down / 110

The Other Side of the Fence / 112

The Cutting Edge / 113

Showers / 114

Fasting / 116

7. THE CIRCLE OF LIFE / 119

The Lizard / 120

Her Final Gift / 121

Small Things / 122

A Bad Day / 124

Advent Resurrection / 125

The Other Side of the Hill / 126

Plotting the Resurrection / 127

Contents

The Barbershop / 129

I Forgot / 130

Easter Afterglow / 131

8. OUR DAILY LIFE / 133

One Person Is Missing / 133

Just Do It / 135

If I Were God… / 136

Miracles / 137

Words to Live By / 139

The Hole in the Window / 140

Neighbors / 141

The Broken Places / 143

Generous Eyes / 145

The Light / 147

The Survivors / 148

Reboot / 150

99.9 Percent the Same / 152

Spoiled! / 153

Daily Bread / 155

"Please Touch the Flowers" / 156

9. THE SEASONS / 159

Shadows / 160

Wheat / 161

Late Bloomers / 162

Epiphany / 163

The Dark / 165

Spring Forward / 166

Sunsets / 168

Finding God in the Midst of the Mess / 169

The Snowman / 170

Hope / 171

Let Him Easter in Us / 173

Stuck! / 173

Introduction

This book is a collection of columns I have written through the years. Several thousand people receive the weekly column by e-mail, and I'm finally responding to many ongoing requests by readers for a book.

This is a compilation of brief stories. When I first got serious about publishing them, I thought of them as "my" stories. However, as I have lived with them in manuscript form over the past few months, there has been a dawning clarity that they aren't my stories at all.

Here is my progression of thought: after acknowledging to myself that they weren't really *my* stories, I assumed that they were *your* stories, somehow conveyed to me as I have wandered through life. Now, after a considerable amount of time pondering this, I think I have figured out what seems to be the obvious yet nevertheless elusive truth: they are *our* stories. We share them because *we* have lived them.

That's always the case, isn't it? If a story is good, it conveys an experience, a truth, a mystery, or a question that life has placed before you. That's the way it was from the very beginning when someone first read to you about a fairy princess and you knew that princess because she was you, or you knew about the fiery dragon because he, or something similar, had haunted your dreams.

The stories in this book, of course, are not made up. I once started a novel, somehow deluded by the belief that I could make up a story that would be interesting enough to read. I was astonished to discover that I'm not very good at making up such tales. I assume that all those years of preaching have somehow eroded any talent I might have had for fiction. Preaching, after all, is at least partially the art of convincing people that what you have to say is fact, not fiction.

What I am reasonably good at is *noticing*. I was first tempted to say that I am good at observing, but that doesn't quite convey the meaning I have in mind. Noticing, at least to me, means not only observing but also thinking about the meaning of that which has been observed. (I am indebted to my friend Dr. Alyce McKenzie for my appreciation of this term. She writes a wonderful blog titled "Knack for Noticing.")

I want to return to a phrase I used in the third paragraph of this introduction. The phrase "somehow conveyed to me as I have wandered through life" is one of those statements that just flowed out of my fingers and onto the keyboard as I was typing. It is a statement that has haunted me somewhat as I have tried to finish this introduction, and that is always a clue for me that I should "take notice."

I think the truth is that we do wander through life. All of our attempts at getting out the map and plotting our course are always thwarted by the detours life throws at us (see chapter 1). I have occasionally asked a sanctuary full of people to consider it this way: "Think for a moment about your very earliest memory. Where were you at the time? Now think about that long, winding road that brought you from that place to this place and to this moment. Was that God or was that luck?"

Anyone who has been around for a while and who goes

through this thought exercise will be overwhelmed by the twists and turns of that long, winding road that has been one's journey through life. No way to plot it; no way to control those things that were unplanned and unexpected. But we can think about them and their meaning and, in so doing, attempt to weave a richer and more colorful tapestry of understanding, or perhaps just appreciation, for the journey.

So maybe that is the best we can do. Embrace the questions and the mystery. Celebrate the journey, even the painful parts. And take notice along the way that God has somehow been present.

Finally, a word is warranted about the title. A few years ago I was able to buy a few acres of pasture land near Gainesville, Texas, not too far south of the Oklahoma border. I fenced it, built a small barn with an apartment in it, and bought a few cows to inhabit the place along with my two horses. It is more a retreat than a ranch, but it partially fulfilled my lifelong dream of being a "rancher." An unexpected gift of Siete Ranch has been the inspiration it has provided for sermons and columns, and the "thinking time" that has been provided by the one-hour commute back and forth from my home in Plano, Texas.

And so I offer these reflections to you as little gifts to ponder as you make your own way through life. It would please me greatly if, every now and then, one of these stories were to spark an insight or perhaps even some very personal kind of epiphany about your own journey. At the very least, I hope you will draw the conclusion that you have a good traveling companion who is pleased to share the trail with you.

About the Siete Brand

I am often asked about Siete Ranch and where the name came from. You will probably not be surprised to learn that there is a story that goes with the answer.

Years ago I bought a nice sorrel gelding from a legendary cowboy by the name of Roe Miller. Roe, a member of the Big Bend Cowboy Hall of Fame, had retired to Fort Davis in far west Texas, and we became friends. This horse was branded on the left hip with his Siete brand—a Spanish "seven"—and I admired its simplicity.

In most western states brands are registered with the state, but in Texas brands are registered with the county. As a courtesy I asked Roe if he minded if I registered the brand in the counties north of Dallas where I've had cows and horses through the years. As a practical matter, more than five hundred miles were separating my livestock and his, so he seemed pleased for me to register his brand.

When I bought the property I was fussing with what to

name it, and my good friend Jan Davis suggested Siete Ranch. I remember telling her I didn't think it made sense. "Why would one name a place 'Seven Ranch'?" Her retort was, as usual, pretty compelling: "This is supposed to be a place of rest for you. God rested on the seventh day. Siete Ranch is the perfect name." End of story.

I buried Roe Miller in the old Fort Davis cemetery a number of years ago. It was the real cowboy deal with his brand burned into a pine box and his boots and spurs placed backward in the stirrups of his saddle. His old horse was whinnying. You can't tell me that cowboys don't cry. I like to think of Roe up there looking down from heaven, pretty darned proud that his beloved Siete brand still lives on in this book.

Chapter 1

The Journey

I have often said that there are two kinds of people: those who are on a spiritual journey and know it, and those who are on a spiritual journey but don't know it yet. I believe that the spiritual journey includes the quest for meaning, the search for God, and the hunger for significant relationships. That quest continues until our dying day.

It is human nature to think that we can arrive at the destination of our choosing on the timetable that is most convenient. We strive for the big achievements in life—graduation, marriage, children, the big job or promotion, great wealth—thinking each time that we have finally "arrived." In a very real sense, many of us remain captive to the fairy tale of "living happily ever after" when, in fact, the journey never ends. Each step must have its own meaning, and we must strive to find joy in the direction of our lives rather than in the destination.

This group of reflections includes some thoughts on how our journey sometimes takes us on detours to places we think we don't want to go. But, if we are thoughtful and observant, we will often find that there are great lessons to be learned from life's detours. Even when we are completely lost, we may stumble onto some of life's greatest blessings. Just as getting lost on a country drive may take you by some incredibly scenic spot you otherwise would never have seen, there are times of great personal discoveries when you feel emotionally or spiritually lost. Those are some of the things I contemplate on drives between my city home and my little ranch in north Texas.

7- The Road, Part 1

A long, hot, dry Texas summer had decimated FM 1385, the paved county highway I travel regularly. Most of the road was fine, but there were sections where the base under the road had collapsed. To get past those sections I had to slow to less than forty miles per hour, and even then it often felt more like sailing a small boat over high seas than driving. If there was oncoming traffic, it could be dangerous.

Coming home one night I couldn't help thinking about how my journeys across that road were emblematic of my trek through life. Sometimes my life's path has been straight and true and smooth, with no real obstacles. There have been times when it was easy travelin' and I made good time toward my destination. Other times I have hit rough patches that slowed me down, turbulence that frightened me, and discomfort that tempted me to give up.

I drove that county road so often that I knew where the bad spots were. They didn't bother me much. I knew that it wouldn't be far before things smoothed out. Whenever I neared a bad section, I would remind myself to slow down, drive carefully, and be patient.

You know where this is heading. Wisdom does not come easily, especially the kind that allows us to understand the length and scope of the journey God has laid in front of us. Looking back on my life, I wish I could have displayed more equanimity during my rough patches. I'd like to say that I always knew things would smooth out, but I didn't. I certainly didn't always understand it at an emotional and spiritual level. Sometimes I railed against the injustice of life; sometimes I panicked. There were times when I simply cried.

I would also like to say that I have learned my lesson and that I now not only fully understand the inevitability of tough times but also trust the good news that things will always get better. I can't tell you that. I'm sure there will be times to come when I will again rail against injustice or will panic or weep. Such are the limitations of my human nature. But I hope that I am slowly becoming wiser and that, when faced with such temptations, I will be reminded of what FM 1385 has taught me: slow down, travel carefully, and be patient. Things are going to get better.

7- The Road, Part 2

I had so many responses to the column about my adventures along FM 1385 that I decided to do a sequel. I was traveling with my four-year-old grandson several weeks after writing that column, and we passed a section where there was a detour sign. Liam was at that age where he asked about anything and wanted to understand everything. So the question came: "What does that sign say?" I told him, and he followed with the inevitable, "What is a detour?"

Have you tried explaining a detour to a four-year-old? I won't attempt to replicate that conversation, but I do want to tell you that it nudged forward my memories of some of the detours I've taken through the years. It seems that we are never really receptive to detours. Let's face it, they cost us time and sometimes money. Yet I have fond recollections of country roads and back-country scenery I would never have enjoyed had it not been for the unanticipated side trips.

I also remember some of the detours I have encountered professionally and personally. In fact, most of my life-changing moments have come in ways that were unexpected. When you are traveling down one road, you don't anticipate suddenly turning in a direction that was not on your map—mental or otherwise. At the time, some of my personal detours seemed good, but some appeared to be awful. Honestly, some of them were truly painful. But what is true about them all is that somehow God was working in my life to get me to where I finally needed to be. Looking back, that part is indisputable.

I think I'm going to preach a sermon one day on the importance of detours in life. The working title is "Detours: How God Improves Your Life by Messing It Up." If you give the subject some thought, I'm betting that you will agree with me. God guides us to where we need to be through unexpected and sometimes painful detours from the path we have chosen.

So, wherever you are in life at this moment, take the time to look at the scenery and enjoy the journey. You are not lost because God knows exactly where you are and has every intention of getting you to exactly where you need to be.

7- Confession

Just shy of my sixty-third birthday, I began coming to grips with a personal flaw that I could no longer ignore or pretend was not there. Frankly, it was a private sin, and one about which I had never felt the need to make a public confession. Nevertheless, I came to the conclusion that such an admission would do me good and that, even more, it might be helpful to those who share the same weakness.

It's difficult for me to type these words, but the truth I had to face was that I have a profound distrust *of* God. Perhaps more accurately it was a profound lack of trust *in* God, which may be a sin that is one shade less egregious. As a pastor who has preached for forty years about the importance of trusting God, however, I realized that the difference was relatively minor. Although I had been vaguely aware of this absence of trust all of my life, its consequences were becoming ever more apparent to me as I struggled with the everyday challenges of life.

My epiphany came because of concerns for my grandsons. One afternoon, while plotting all of the many things I needed to do to make sure my two grandsons would be kept safe, raised in a happy home with good moral standards, receive better-than-average educations, and have a head start in life, it occurred to me that I had limited power to ensure that any of those become reality. I heard God speaking to me—a phrase I rarely use because I think it is so often abused by preachers—in a distinctly powerful way. God said, quite simply, "You need to trust some of this to me."

And thus began the argument.

I started off by reminding God of all the children I have buried during my ministry, every one an innocent victim of some awful catastrophe. "Do you really expect *me*, of all people, to trust my grandsons to *you*?" I then proceeded to charge God with negligence over the number of children who are raised in homes that provide inadequate emotional support, in communities and schools with inferior educational opportunities, and in societies that seem impervious to the needs of the next generation. "In all honesty, God, when it comes to my grandsons, I think I can trust myself to get things done better and faster than you."

God was silent. For a long time. At first, sensing that perhaps I had won the debate, I felt moderately triumphant. After a while, however, as God remained silent, I became overwhelmed by the recognition of my utter impotence. Not that I am unable to love my grandchildren, provide money for their education, or help them in many other ways that are appropriate and useful. But I faced the reality of my total powerlessness when it comes to achieving the ultimate goal for those whom I love: a safe life with a maximum of love and a minimum of fear, a life well-lived and long, and a life with more joy than grief, more laughter than tears.

The silence was deafening, the epiphany torturous. Confronted with this sin, which I realized had dogged me all my life, I waited for God's next word. It did not come. Or at least it did not come directly, but only as an echo of a statement God had already made: "You need to trust some of this to me."

And thus ended the argument.

7- Pray

Sitting just outside the open-air tabernacle, I struck up a conversation with the grandmother sitting next to me. "How old is your grandson?" I asked, referring to the little boy she was holding. "Two," she said, an answer I was expecting, but it proved to be a good conversation starter and an opportunity for me to play with the toddler a bit.

As the worship service started at the Bloys Camp Meeting outside Fort Davis, Texas, the little boy's father came up and took the seat on the other side of his mother and son. Sixty minutes later the service came to a close, and the two-year-old had done as well as could be expected. The preacher announced the final benediction, "Let us pray." I closed my eyes and bowed my head, but was suddenly distracted by words being said to my left. I looked over to see that this child's father, a tall, rugged cowboy, had stood and was leaning down to take the little hands of his son and push them together in the familiar fashion of offering prayer. The cowboy was whispering to his son, "Pray. Pray."

I fought back a tear as I realized how profound a moment I had witnessed: a father with no seminary training and probably minimal knowledge of the latest parenting skills, nevertheless starting his young son on his lifelong journey with God. The greatest preacher or theologian in the country couldn't have done a better job. I couldn't help thinking that old Dr. Bloys, who started this Camp Meeting in 1890, would be pleased at how well his work is continuing to be done.

Sometimes I fear that in today's modern world we have made things more complicated than they have to be. We worry about our children, and we go to extraordinary measures and great expense to make sure they are safe and prepared for the challenges that lie ahead. But it may be that the most important experience we can give them is the simplest: Hold their little hands together and begin to teach them the power of prayer.

7- The Café

"How's your mama?" asked the waitress as she sat at the table next to mine, joining the man who had become her customer. "Fine," he said, "how's yours?" I was sitting in a little café in Clarendon, Texas, about one hour east of Amarillo.

The population of Clarendon is about two thousand. A Methodist minister and his followers, all teetotalers, founded the community in the 1870s. Because the locals allowed no drinking or gambling, the cowboys and ranchers in the surrounding territory derisively referred to the town as Saints' Roost. Today it is the home of Clarendon Community College, and it lays claim to a drive-in theater that is open all year long and shows first-run movies. When I was there it was playing *Cars 2*, which I thought was an appropriately family-oriented selection given the town's no-gambling, no-drinking history.

Back to my café story. I couldn't help thinking about the remarkable virtues of small-town life: a young waitress who knows her customers and who takes the leisure to sit with them a moment and ask about their family. A customer who thinks this is not at all unusual. This is what I call real social networking. I don't know what the relationship is between the two of them, but having lived in a small town before, I can guess. It no doubt involves an extensive multi-generational web of family and friends, shared history including skeletons in the closet no one talks about, and genuine mutual affection that accrues in the lives of those who have been neighbors for as long as they can remember.

I have said this many times in recent years: You can Facebook and use Twitter all you want, but in the final analysis there is a fundamental human need to socialize in ways that lie on this side of the digital divide. I know people have made billions in the social network stocks, but in the long term I'm betting on things like face-to-face conversations, holding hands, looking another human being in the eye, and laughing—or sometimes crying—together.

This is just the truth: As long as human beings live and love and hope and care about one another, there will always be a place where people can ask, "How's your mama?"

7- Dreams

One night not too long ago, I wore myself out trying to complete a college final exam for which I was ill-prepared. Even though I was asleep, the experience was about as real as it can get. I awakened from this nightmare in a sweat at 5:45 AM, which is late for me. It was a horrible experience! I'm sure it reflects some of my deep-seated insecurities.

Sometimes we feel ill-prepared for life, don't we? We try to educate ourselves, try to plan and anticipate the challenges that might lie in front of us. We recruit people to help, and we pray.

Still, no matter how much we work at it, we find ourselves over our heads. I'm sure there are some people who are confident this will never happen to them, but I am not one of them. I'm guessing you're not either.

Occasionally I have other dreams, equally powerful but much more enjoyable. For years I have dreamed of being with a group of people who, after crossing a difficult and dangerous valley, make an arduous climb to the top of a ridge. The journey is so difficult I am reluctant to start, but I have been there before and know the trip is worth it. When we get to the top of the ridge, we see what is, quite literally, indescribable beauty. I'm pretty sure that we are looking at eternity. Or perhaps at God.

I wish there were some way we could choose our dreams—just dial up the ones we want each night before we go to sleep. Even though my "journey dream" is demanding, I would choose it often because the rewards are so great. Unfortunately, that's not how the brain works.

But I can tell you this: We *do* get to choose which dreams to pursue in our waking hours, and there is an enormous amount of power and freedom invested in that choice. We can dream of a world where people love God and serve others; we can dream of a generation that works to build a better life for those to come; we can dream of a world at peace. And we can choose to help turn those dreams into reality.

7- The Railroad Truck

I drove to the Tiger Mart in Pilot Point, Texas, one day, and there it was, sitting in front of the store. It was a pickup truck.

But not just an ordinary pickup. It said "Union Pacific" on the doors and, in addition to the four rubber tires, there was a set of elevated steel wheels that allowed the vehicle to run on railroad tracks. I have seen these trucks on many occasions running along the tracks, but this was my first time to see one up close. I admit I was fascinated.

Sometimes, as I am crossing the railroad tracks that lie just to the west of Highway 377, I take a moment and glance down the tracks in both directions. The tracks fascinate me, stretching endlessly (or so it seems) to the north and the south. I remember riding the train as a boy, and the sound and feel of the tracks beneath me.

As I sat there and contemplated this truck with railroad wheels, there was a moment when my mind wandered into fantasy. I imagined turning my truck north or south and just following the tracks as far as they go. An endless journey into the vast beauties and mysteries of the landscape. A journey without traffic congestion or stoplights or complicated directions provided by some Internet mapping site.

I often talk about the concept of journey in my sermons, and I don't think there is any better biblical image for life than that of journey. Beginning with Abraham and continuing with all the patriarchs, Moses, and down to the journey that Mary and Joseph took to Bethlehem, the Bible speaks about life that is fluid and changing, always calling us into the unknown. How we wish it could be as easy and straight and uncomplicated as those railroad tracks! In reality, our spiritual journeys are more like the ones we take in our automobiles with the complicated maps: congestion on the interstate, a wrong turn here, a detour there. Even most of our biblical heroes experienced the challenges of finding their way through life.

There is hope. The Old Testament speaks of the Lord who will one day make the path straight. I believe that will be the case. Meanwhile, we are in this together, and the journey can even be fun and invigorating if you have the right traveling companions.

7 Fog

Several weeks ago I was driving through the hills southwest of Fort Worth. It was quite early in the morning, and I was treated to a gorgeous sight: dense fog had accumulated in the low places. It is a rare Texas morning when you can top a hill on a highway and look upon vast clouds that have gathered in the valleys. I was struck by the way the fog had settled, leaving clear visibility at the higher elevations. It was an interesting drive, descending into dense fog with little visibility, and then rising above the clouds into a clear sky.

It occurred to me that life is very similar. It is usually in the low places in life where we have the most difficulty seeing our paths and finding our way. When we are dealing with grief, stress, or depression, it is indeed as if fog has clouded our vision, leaving us with few clues about where we are going or the turns in life we should take.

As I've thought about it, it seems to me that the rules for driving through fog are pretty relevant for navigating through the crises in life:

1. Go slow. Take your time. Speed only compounds the risk.

2. Take one step at a time. Fog only allows you to see the next step, but once you've taken it, the next one will then be visible.

3. Be persistent. Know that, down the road and above the fog, there is a clear sky and a shining sun.

If you take one step at a time, you will eventually climb out of the valley and break free of the fog.

Chapter 2

Inspiring Lives

I've often said that I believe in luck, both good and bad. I also believe in blessings from God, and sometimes it's hard for me to decide between what is God-given and what is the luck of the draw.

I know I am both lucky and blessed to have a wonderful family. My grandparents were extraordinary human beings. One grandfather was a farmer and preacher from Tennessee, the other a stern but loving Texas lawman. He spent most of his career as a Deputy Sheriff of Dallas County, but also spent time as a Texas Ranger. He once arrested the famous Depression era gangster Clyde Barrow, thereby becoming one of the few men to do so and live to tell about it.

The women in my life were strong, hard working, loving, and religious. They taught me values that have served me my whole life, especially as I married and had children and grand-children of my own. Whenever I write about members of my family, it is a powerful reminder that their blood runs in my veins, and that is a tremendous source of encouragement.

I even had the best in-laws ever. I don't know how much was luck and how much was God, but it is clear I have been extraordinarily blessed.

In this chapter I share some stories about family members, friends, and mentors who deserve none of the blame for my many mistakes, but much of the credit for whatever I have accomplished and learned in life. I've even included a little known story about James Bonham that has always inspired me. Every time I read through these I say a little prayer of thanksgiving for them and so many others. I hope I have properly honored them with these memories and recollections.

7 Sacrifice

My father-in-law, Bill Thompson, was a great man. A member of what is known as the Greatest Generation, he died at age eighty-seven. As a veteran of the Army's legendary 36th Division, he survived several amphibious landings and five major campaigns. He landed in Italy among the first American troops to set foot in Europe in WWII and fought in some of the toughest battles of the war.

I think about Bill during the Lenten season because of the concept of sacrifice that we speak of so often these days. The idea of giving up something for Lent would have seemed absurd to Bill simply because he had already given up most of the things the rest of us pursue. While hunkering down in a foxhole in the middle of Italy, he arrived at the conclusion that he, like so many of his comrades, would never come home alive. "If I do," he told God, "all I will ever ask for is the opportunity to catch a fish, cook a hamburger on an open fire, and take care of my family."

Lots of people say it; few live it. Quite simply, he did. Till the day he died, his only real possessions, other than a few clothes, were the shotgun he had inherited from his father, his pocket knife, and his old rod and reel. He didn't need or want anything else. He drove and maintained his cars until they were nothing but rust buckets with springs coming up through the seats. He had no desire to travel to Europe ("I've been there already.") or eat at fancy restaurants ("How can you beat the catfish we fry in the backyard? We eat like kings!"). Birthdays and Christmases were always challenges for the rest of us because he truly didn't want or need anything.

So the question I'm pondering is the meaning of sacrifice. While I believe that giving up sweets, alcohol, or potato chips for forty days is a meaningful spiritual discipline, I wonder about what it means to truly sacrifice for someone else in the way that the Greatest Generation did for us or in the way that Jesus did for humanity. I have listened carefully to the political/social debate that rages in our country. Basically I hear from most people that they believe in sacrifice as long as someone else is the one who is making it.

Today I think about the boys who left their farms and the girls who went to the factories, about the food shortages and the waiting lines, and about the ones who never came home. I think about how almost everything we have, including our freedom, is because of a generation that didn't bother to ask "why me?" when called upon to sacrifice. There are brave, self-sacrificing soldiers in every generation. Still, compared to that generation, many of us are failing the test of what it means to be American. I'm hoping that can be reversed before our children sit down to write a column about my generation.

7 Hats

I own a number of hats. Among them are several straw hats I wear in the summer months. One of them is nicer than the others, and I reserve it for special occasions. I also have some felt hats I wear in the cooler months or when it is raining. There's a really nice one that was custom made for me by a hatter in Alpine, Texas, and it even has my name printed on the inside sweat band.

My favorite hat is an old silver-belly Stetson that belonged to my father. It is rather crumpled and beat up. It has a hole in it, and it has lots of sweat stains. In spite of how it looks, it is my favorite hat because some of those sweat stains are mine, and some of them are his. He died many years ago, but sometimes when I put on his hat I can look in the mirror and see his blue eyes. There are moments when I think I can smell his aftershave as if he were standing right there next to me. When I go to check on the horses or cows, I remember the times I went with him when he was wearing that hat. Sometimes I pretend we are walking through the pasture together, and I remember how much he liked looking at white-faced Hereford cattle in a green meadow.

They say hats are good for you because they keep the sun off your face and off those bald places on your scalp. They also help keep your hair dry when it is raining. Sometimes a hat will also impart a certain sense of style, which is something that I desperately need. But I like this hat because it is a hat full of memories.

7- Big Spur

That's what he was known as to several generations of kids who, under his tutelage, learned to ride a horse, shoot a bow and arrow, and camp in the mountains that he so loved. He was nicknamed Big Spur, and he was a legend bigger than life.

I was twelve the first time I rode with him. He was fifty-six. I will never forget riding into a meadow cradled between the peaks of two mountains. We stopped, and from horseback he looked around and surveyed the ranch land on which he had been born. I could see in his eyes that he loved every rock, every blade of grass, every cactus. And then he took his hat off and said, "Let's pray." And that he did, confirming my adolescent speculation that he was mighty pleased with God for the gift of beauty into which he had been born, and for which he would be eternally grateful.

John G. "Big Spur" Prude died at the age of ninety-five. His memorial service was the following Sunday in the little Methodist church of Fort Davis. I didn't hear about it until the following Monday evening, or I would have been there to pay a final tribute to this giant of a man who served as patriarch of a great family and as a role model to literally thousands of boys and girls who never forgot him even as they themselves became parents and grandparents.

The last time I saw Big Spur was at the Bloys Camp Meeting on the road between Fort Davis and Valentine. I knew he had quit riding horses a year or so earlier, and he had just come out of the hospital. He was a bit frail, but he greeted me with the same enormous enthusiasm I had come to expect over the past thirty-nine years. He could always make you feel special.

John Prude lived his life the same way he rode his horses: tall and proud, graceful, never holding on but always perfectly balanced and in harmony with the One who would get him where he wanted to go. Those who are left behind can't mourn too much because we know the joy he has now experienced at having arrived at that final destination, which had been in his plans for so many years. Nevertheless, I suspect that in my dreams I will see a horse with no rider making his way through the mountains of Prude Ranch and be reminded once again of the terrible loss that has fallen upon the land and the people he loved so much.

7- John Bengel

From time to time I like to do some reminiscing. And so, I want to share a story about someone I've spoken of but never written about. He was the father of one of my high school classmates and a close friend of my father. His name was John Bengel.

John Bengel was a building contractor and tough as a boot. He did not mince his words, which were often sprinkled with mild profanity; if you stepped out of line when around him, you were sure to be called down. His son was the star quarterback of the high school football team, and so there were always lots of football players around. We all thought we were tough, but we melted in the presence of Mr. Bengel.

Here is the part I've never told before: in the three years and nine months that I knew him, he became one of my childhood heroes. He was perhaps the most generous man I have ever known. He had made money, and he had lost money, but for him money was nothing more than an opportunity to be generous with his church, community, family, and friends. Even as a sixteen-year-old, I figured out that he had a heart as big as Texas.

My father once told me that most people in Denison did not know that John would go quietly to the hospital to visit those who were ill. Without fanfare he would lend or give money to someone who was in need. For many, many years now, John Bengel has exemplified for me what it means to live generously.

After I moved from Denison, Mr. Bengel was diagnosed with cancer. He lost part of his brain and a section of his skull, which was replaced by a steel plate. He lost his business, most of his money, and in his final years he was dramatically underemployed. But he never lost his place in my mind and heart. He remains one of my heroes.

He died a number of years ago. He was never a perfect human being, but I have no doubt that he ended up on the right side of the pearly gates. I hope he's listening in because, after all these years, I figure it's time for me to say, "Thank you. You lived the good life, and you taught me what it means to live generously." What better legacy could one leave behind?

7 · One Last Call

I was going through my Contacts folder in Microsoft Outlook one morning trying to find a name. There are often more than 800 names in that file, so occasionally, when I am going through it, I will delete outdated names and addresses. As I deleted a name here and there, I came upon an entry that both startled me and brought a tear to my eye: Bill Thompson. There was no e-mail address, but his mobile phone number was listed, and I thought about how much I would like to talk with him.

I remember the first time I saw him. I was twenty-seven years old and standing in the pulpit of one of my denomination's churches in Frisco, Texas. A man in his early fifties walked into the back of the sanctuary, dressed in a dark suit, a white shirt, a dark tie. I took one look at him and immediately thought, "That is the toughest man I ever laid eyes on." Looks were not deceiving. In the ensuing years we spent thousands of hours hunting and fishing together and, though he was my senior by almost thirty years, I could never keep up with him. An outdoorsman at heart, he had less need for the comforts of life than any human being I've ever known.

Among those who worked with him during his forty-plus years at a major utility company, he was somewhat of a legend, remembered not only for his skill as a welder but for his numerous exploits. To this day the grown children of co-workers talk about the man about whom they heard stories around the dinner table. I doubt that you could find anyone who ever worked with him who would disagree with that "toughest man" description. The stories could fill a book.

The father of four daughters, one of whom I was lucky enough to marry, he placed as the greatest priority in life taking care of his family. Family cookouts with Bill were frequent and grand occasions. Those times spent with Bill are some of the best of my life.

My father-in-law died several years ago at age eighty-seven. He was a World War II hero, a great father, and as good a father-in-law as a man could ever have. If God had given me a chance to pick the perfect father-in-law, it would have been Bill.

I was tempted to think about what it would be like to dial him up and hear his voice one more time. Reluctantly, I pushed the "Delete" button. There was no more need for that phone number. Even as I write this, however, I am second-guessing myself, wishing I had dialed it one more time. Did Bill have a recording on that number? Do you suppose it is still active? I know the answers: He didn't have a recording, and it wouldn't still be active even if he had. But I still wish I had dialed it one last time.

Bill Thompson would have been the first person to tease me about this. He wasn't big on technology, and he had little need for the material things most of us crave. He only had a mobile phone in his last year of life so he could call one of his girls from the nursing home in case of an emergency. Bill would have flipped the ash from his cigarette, grinned, and said, "Don, you haven't deleted me from your heart. That's what counts." And he would have been right.

7- Bonham

The first week of March is an important time if you are a Texan, transplanted or otherwise. March 2, 1836, is the day Texas declared its independence. March 6 is the anniversary of the day the Alamo fell in 1836 at approximately 6:30 AM.

When someone asks me, "What's the big deal about being Texan?" I ask if they've visited the Alamo. Despite how one might feel about Texans, or about being a Texan, the inevitable emotion that surfaces on the grounds of the Alamo is humility. I've seen grown men try to hide their tears as they wander around the premises; in fact, that might be more the rule than the exception.

One of the lesser known Alamo stories is that of James Butler Bonham, who made a number of trips by horseback out of the fort carrying Colonel William B. Travis's requests for reinforcements. Travis was the twenty-six-year-old commander who, in a letter, vowed to defend the Alamo with his life. Bonham was consistently turned down, with one inspired exception: a group of thirty-two Texans who had gathered at Gonzales, moved by the recited words of Travis, responded by riding to the Alamo and fighting their way inside so that they might die in honor defending what they believed in.

In his book *Lone Star*, noted Texas historian T. R. Fehrenbach tells of the last recorded words of Bonham:

"At the very end, the weary Bonham, a lawyer, a Carolinian of exalted family, and a friend of Travis, turned his mount around and rode back toward San Antonio. He was told it was useless to throw away his life. He answered that Buck Travis deserved to know the answer to his appeals, spat upon the ground, and galloped west into his own immortality." (Da Capo Press, 2000; 211.)

The defense of the Alamo was, at the time, not a parochial story. Those who died inside those fabled walls included citizens of most of the states and of Mexico: Anglos, African Americans, and Hispanics. As with the storming of the Bastille in 1789, the story quickly became a global one that inspired the lovers and defenders of freedom around the world. Words such as *courage* and *honor* took on new meaning, and the result was an enlarged vision of what ordinary human beings are capable of when standing for the common good.

Today, in places around the world, men, women, and children are, at the risk of life and limb, making their stand for freedom. They are at times outnumbered, and certainly outgunned, but their opponents cannot match them in terms of courage, honor, and passion. They are the legacy of James Butler Bonham and countless others who believed that the right to be free and live in dignity is God-given.

I don't know about you but, at the risk of being criticized for the Texan thing, I always take a private moment on March 6 at 6:30 AM to remember the Alamo and those who gave all they had for freedom.

7- A Father's Sacrifice

Roy Smith was a great preacher of a previous generation. He told a story about his father, a man who had been a hard-working farmer all his life. Soon after starting college, Roy returned home after hearing of his father's unexpected death. Going through his father's few possessions, he found his father's shoes and noticed there were enormous holes in both of them. Looking at those shoes he broke into tears and sobbed because only two weeks earlier his father had bought him a brand new pair of shoes to wear to college. It was then he realized how much his father had sacrificed for him.

A number of years ago, I was going through an old file cabinet and found some papers that had belonged to my father. Among them was a bank loan marked "paid in full." As I read the terms of the loan, I discovered that my father had made the note way back in the 1960s in order to pay for my college tuition. The biggest surprise was to see the date of the final payment that had been made years after my graduation. My father died when I was thirty-nine years old, and in all those years he never said a single word about that bank loan. Like Roy Smith, I broke down and cried.

Most of us like to think that we are self-made, believing we have earned and deserve what we have. But someplace along the line someone bought you the shoes to wear to school or packed the lunch you carried with you. Someone helped with the tuition at college or spent valuable time teaching and mentoring you about life and work. Who was the teacher who accepted the wages of a public servant in order to give you the skills to make more money than she could have ever dreamed of? We all stand on the shoulders of others who made sacrifices for us.

I have never doubted that my father was a great man. But his greatness cannot be measured by the size of his estate, which was modest, nor by his professional accomplishments, which were enormous. His true greatness, like that of many others of his generation, can be measured only by his commitment to leave for his children a better and more decent world. I pray that my generation will gain the courage to follow their example before it is too late.

7 Johnny

One of the most powerful memories of my early childhood is of a little boy in my first grade class in the little town of McKenzie, Tennessee. He was different from the rest of us. He looked different. He acted differently. He obviously had enormous challenges. For some reason, almost sixty years later, I think of him often. It is a memory that haunts me.

What I now know—and at some level I think I knew even then—is that he was the product of excruciating poverty. The reason he looked and acted differently is that he was malnourished. He did not consume enough calories to physically and mentally keep up with the rest of us. I dare not speculate on how well he was emotionally nurtured by his parents.

Now in my sixties, I am very clear and very focused on the fact that the future of our country—the future of humanity—depends on how well we are feeding and teaching and nurturing our children. We have teachers who are doing what I consider to be heroic work; we have churches and social agencies that are committed to helping and nurturing children; we have many parents who are as devoted as parents can be. In spite of that, our collective report card is horrendous.

If you pay attention to the statistics, you can't help being concerned about the number of children who are growing up in dangerous and chaotic neighborhoods, being reared in unstable family systems, attending schools not equipped to give them what they need, and relying on inadequate healthcare and nutrition. The trajectory of this trend is a nosedive. It is getting worse, not better.

This is not a political statement. I will leave it to the pundits and politicians to fight it out about who has the best policy plan for addressing these issues. No, this is about you and me. The truth is that many of us don't act in a way that demonstrates that we care about these children. Many of us who are Baby Boomers appear to be more concerned about our retirement than what is taking place in the ill-equipped school across town. We tend to focus on our future rather than the future of those who will come after us.

There are people who, understandably, will advise not talking about a problem unless you have an answer. Well, the first part of the answer is to admit that we have a problem. And next, we should stop blaming people on the other side of the political divide. The problem belongs to us all, and answers will emerge when we decide to unite rather than divide, to admit rather than alibi or blame, to act rather than postpone.

That little boy's name was Johnny. I was not his friend. I avoided him because I did not understand or feel comfortable around him. Six decades have passed and I, for one, need to make up for lost time.

7 A Dog Story

Sometimes my brain just stops working and I have to find a way of unlocking what little intelligence and creativity might be left up there. Some people call it writer's block. Whatever it is, it happened yesterday as I found myself working simultaneously on both a sermon and this column. My go-to move is to jump in the truck and drive around, usually to one of our wonderful public parks. I don't know why driving helps thaw my brain, but most of the time it works. So that's how I found myself driving through Russell Creek Park yesterday evening around 5:45 PM.

As I drove over one of those huge speed bumps that seem to slow my truck down to less than one mph, I saw a man walking two large black dogs through the park. One of them had what appeared to be bicycle training wheels attached to his hind legs. I don't really know the reason for this, but I assumed that the hind legs of this dog were either paralyzed or otherwise injured. I was fascinated as I watched him running ahead of his owner and even outpacing the other dog, which appeared to be healthy.

The other day I saw a news video about a young woman who has no arms but who has been licensed to fly an airplane. Her capacity to adapt what she has to what she needs is just amazing. She can fly, she can paint, and she can even put on her eye makeup using only her toes and feet. As you know, there are thousands of stories like this, stories that reveal the triumph of human spirit and ingenuity over amazing odds.

I am just haunted by the thought that if we are smart and courageous enough, what we have is all we need. I think about our political leaders. If ordinary human beings can create ways to make paralyzed dogs ambulatory, and if a teenager can fly an airplane with her feet, surely our leaders can be courageous enough and creative enough and (dare I say it?) collaborative enough to lead us into a new vision that encompasses possibilities about how to thrive as individuals and as nations.

Of course, that might require the rest of us to also be brave, creative, and adaptive. We might even have to explore the question of whether or not we are capable of matching the courage and attitude of a common dog.

7 Miracle on the Hudson

Newspapers were full of exuberant quotations. One passenger said, "He has done something great for the human family." Another remarked, "This is the greatest day of my life." New York Governor David Paterson said, "We had a 'Miracle on 34th Street.' I believe now we have had a Miracle on the Hudson" (The Associated Press, January 16, 2009).

The praise for Captain "Sully" Sullenberger can be found everywhere. Ordinarily, I would not write about an event that has been as well publicized as this one, but I make an exception for the simple reason that Captain Sullenberger is connected to the church I pastor. He grew up in Denison, Texas, just sixty miles north of here, and graduated from Denison High School three years behind me. My father was his pastor, and he attended the same youth fellowship that I did.

On Monday I discovered that one of our church members, Mary Wilson, is the sister of Sully Sullenberger. Mary also grew up at Waples Memorial United Methodist Church in Denison. Reminiscing with her about Denison, she made the comment that both she and Sully consider my father to have been their "childhood pastor." Now, forty-six years later, I am her pastor.

It has been striking to observe the nearly universal reaction of the nation to this man and his heroic landing. He not only set a plane down intact in the Hudson River, but as it was sinking he walked the empty cabin twice to make sure no one was left behind, saving every passenger. Standing on the wing of the airplane with other survivors, his reply to their cries of gratitude was a simple and humble, "You're welcome."

In the midst of an awful economic downturn, with horrible news about poorly managed companies and billionaire swindlers, there is much to cheer about this man, his crew, and the equally brave passengers. As Captain Sullenberger's wife said, "I think everybody was ready for some good news."

I maintain that there are more Captain Sullenbergers around than we recognize. There are many who, on a daily basis, help create "good news" with acts of kindness and service, and sometimes unrecognized heroism. At our church we call it simply, "Loving God, Serving Others...Transforming Lives." It's a good motto for any church.

7- Chasing the Big Bucks!

I enjoy the game of golf. One Sunday afternoon I was watching the Tour Championship that was being played at the Olympic Club in San Francisco. At the time it was the largest purse in golf, with the winner receiving more than $500,000. Brad Bryant was not a household name. He was a veteran tour player who had struggled for years to just make a living. But he found himself on the final day of play contending for the richest prize in golf. He was chasing the big bucks, and I must tell you that I was pulling for him.

Brad didn't win the tournament, but he did come in third,

way ahead of most of the greatest names in contemporary golf. He won over $200,000, and I was glad for him. But during the climactic moments of the tournament, when it looked like he had a chance to win, the TV commentators posted a quotation from Brad on the screen. I don't remember it exactly, but this is pretty close: In the end it won't make any difference how much money we make out here. The most important thing will be whether or not we've been good fathers.

I knew I liked that guy! That is such a beautiful example of someone who has his priorities in order. Note that he didn't say that money isn't important—in fact, part of being a good father is paying attention to the physical and financial needs of our families. Nor did he say he didn't care about winning. I watched him that afternoon, and I know that he wanted to win as badly as anyone out there. I'm quite sure he would have had no objections to that $500,000 in prize money. What he said was this: ultimately, our worth and value as human beings will be measured not by how much money we make, but by how we have influenced the lives of others. He was clear about what is ultimately important as opposed to what is important only in the short run.

Part of what the worship experience does for me every Sunday is offer a reminder about the priorities in life. I need that every week because it is so easy to get confused and lost. And part of what the church does for me is to offer an opportunity to invest myself in a way that makes a difference in the lives of others.

I am grateful to Brad Bryant for being my "preacher" on that Sunday afternoon, and for affirming what you and I already know: chasing the big bucks can be both fun and rewarding if we don't forget about what is *really* important in life.

7- Family Reunion

The Hatfields and McCoys are back on speaking terms again. It was a story that rated a prominent article in the *Dallas Morning News* (June 12, 2000).

They gathered at Tug Fork Valley, right on the state line of Kentucky and West Virginia. At first, the Hatfields stayed on the West Virginia side and the McCoys huddled together on the Kentucky side. Slowly, tentatively, the families worked their way to the state line to greet one another, and suddenly it was accomplished. For the first time in a century the two families met peaceably at the site where the legendary feud began over the theft of a pig. After one hundred years and a dozen killings, the families had a prayer together and put the past into the past.

The reunion's organizer, the Reverend Bo McCoy, said this: "It's a bloody past, but we're embracing it. . . . We can't change the past. But life goes on. It's gone on" ("Hatfields, McCoys Joined by Feud," *St. Petersburg Times* OnLine, June 12, 2000). Proof could be found in the group of Hatfields and McCoys huddled together quietly studying a photograph of the 1890 hanging that took the last life lost in the feud. It was a somber moment as they weighed the burden of blood and unnecessary loss of life. Then the reunion turned to happier activities such as hot dogs and a good-natured softball game.

We read about the Hatfields and McCoys and can't help

thinking about those ridiculous, but bloody, feuds all around the globe: the Middle East, Africa, Central Europe. Where does the list end? Almost all of them are about what mountain people call "bad blood." They had their beginnings in some disagreement in history, but they continued because of bad feelings, the desire for vengeance, and the need to even the score. Thousands killed for very little more reason than bad blood. But we read about this reunion, and we wonder if, by the grace of God, it couldn't happen in other places as well. Maybe something as simple as a prayer and the offer to let the past be the past. Some food, a softball game, and a new beginning.

When you really think about it, maybe it could even happen to you and your clan.

7 Saragosa

I first drove through Saragosa, Texas, in the 1960s. It was the first of many, many trips through the wide place in the road between Pecos and Balmorrhea, at the foothills of the Davis Mountains. I have always looked for the dry goods store at the edge of town—a sure sign that I was traveling through Saragosa and that Balmorrhea was only a few miles down the road.

This year I kept looking for the dry goods store—just some small fragment or remains of it—but it was not there. Nothing was there. I was confused. Had I arrived in Saragosa or not? Then I saw the fields on both sides of the road, filled with scattered, twisted steel and demolished vehicles, the work of a deadly tornado. I came to the Red Cross station and the trailers serving as temporary housing, and I knew that I was in what was left of the town.

As much as I had tried to prepare myself for Saragosa, it was nevertheless inadequate. I tried to fight back the tears as we drove past a sign pointing to the cemetery. The thoughts of little children and preschool programs came into my head, and I felt momentarily overwhelmed by grief.

Another chapter, however, is being written in the story of Saragosa. The community will rise out of the ashes and dust, and it will continue to live, because its people will continue to live. Even in the midst of death, Saragosa and its people are discovering life, and the chapter they are now writing is a tribute to the will, determination, and faith of people who will not give up.

There is a remarkable tradition in the Davis Mountains. No matter where you drive, natives who pass you on the road always wave. Always. It is a holdover, I believe, from the days when people had to depend on one another for survival, when the perils of the frontier provided such a common enemy that strangers were united in their quest for safety and survival. That same spirit is alive with those who are rebuilding Saragosa.

Even in the city, there is much that we can learn from the Saragosa natives. We can learn that God's grace does not end with tragedy. We can learn that life is oftentimes a matter of rising out of the ashes of defeat or failure or grief. And we can learn to wave in the knowledge that we really do need one another if we are to survive.

7 Mama

Mama was born in 1901 in Dallas County, a time and place where very few women pursued higher education. By age twenty, however, she had earned a degree in English from Baylor University. She was also fluent in French and a competitive tennis player. She was, by any measure, a remarkable woman.

She married a Texas lawman and lived a simple life, raising a family and always supporting her church. Though she was thoroughly conventional in most ways, I guess she was an early feminist. She always worked outside the home, first as a schoolteacher and then as an assistant for an insurance agency. Looking back I can see that she had enormous energy and easily balanced her home and work life.

Mama, as all her grandkids called her, was forever young, optimistic, and energetic. She loved, supported, and encouraged all of her grandchildren, even those with grandiose schemes (she thought my idea about raising a horse in the backyard of our suburban home in Dallas was a darned good one!). Though I was only twelve when she died of cancer, she—perhaps as much as anyone in my life—had an enormous influence on how I view and live my life.

I was only five or six years old when she taught me her favorite lines of poetry, the opening couplet from Robert Browning's "Rabbi Ben Ezra." I have never forgotten the words, and I share them here with you, along with the rest of the opening stanza. I can't help thinking that Mama would be pleased to know that, after all the passing years, her indomitable spirit and beautiful wisdom lives on.

Grow old along with me!
The best is yet to be,
The last of life, for which the first was made:
Our times are in His hand
Who saith "A whole I planned,
Youth shows but half; trust God: see all, nor be afraid!"

Chapter 3

Memories

I sometimes think I was born in the wrong century, or at least the wrong part of the century. I often regret not getting to ride a horse to school every day or missing out on the old cattle drives.

I remember as a child finding a bridle in my grandfather's garage. I picked it up and felt the leather, smelled it, and knew it to be authentic, well-used, and old. I fantasized about where it had been, the horses it had guided, and the cowboys who had handled it. To me, it was much more valuable than any new bridle I could have picked out at the local feed store.

And so I have a love/hate relationship with modernity. I often wax nostalgic about my childhood and simpler times. So many things I have treasured seem to have disappeared from modern society. I think the world would be better if we had more country roads, small rural towns, and old-time Dairy Queens. But I have learned, reluctantly, to embrace modern technology, and I value the tremendous productivity afforded by computers, cell phones, and other fancy gadgets.

This intersection between the old and the new has been fertile ground for many of my reflections through the years.

7- The Good Old Days

For some reason I started thinking about one of my earliest childhood memories. Like so many such recollections, it seemed insignificant, and yet the imprint it made on my mind is indelible. It revolves around my parents taking my brothers and me to those old-fashioned ice cream drive-ups back in the 1950s.

Back then, before DQ became the huge franchise it is now, there were various names for them—Dairy Bar, Dairy Queen, Dairy Freeze, and so on—but every little town in Texas had one. This was in the days before air-conditioning, and having something cool to eat was always a treat. I also remember they had those yellow lights so as not to attract bugs. We ordered by walking up and talking to someone through a sliding glass window. There was no indoor seating.

I loved almost everything on the menu, but a chocolate milkshake was, without a doubt, my favorite. These milkshakes were way too large for me to finish at that age, and my recent memory was of getting home and placing the remains of one of those shakes in the refrigerator to save for the next day.

A few years ago my wife and our kids traveled to Tennessee with me for a family funeral. On the way back to Texas, I decided to take a detour in order to see some of the tobacco farmland in southern Kentucky. We drove through a little town and, to my delight, there was an independent Dairy Bar on the main road leaving town. I kid you not: it had yellow lights and a sliding glass window. For a moment or two I thought I had been transported back to 1952, and I promise you they delivered the best milkshake I've had in more than fifty years.

Such is the power of memory. We are learning through research that who we become as human beings is a complex mixture of conscious and unconscious adaptation to millions of experiences, beginning at a very young age. I don't fully understand it all, but of one thing I am sure: I want our children to grow up and remember the church as being one of those places where they felt the safest and most joyful. I want them to remember Easter egg hunts and children's songs and the magnificence of the organ and choir. I want them to remember teachers who loved them and taught them important things about life. I want them to drive by fifty years from now, see the steeple, and be filled with warm and tender memories. I want them to tell their grandchildren, "Those were the good ol' days."

7 The Old Icehouse

I attended a meeting in Wichita Falls, Texas, which is where my parents lived when I was in college. I have fond memories of wonderful summers spent there. One evening I took a little sentimental tour and drove around to visit some of the places I remembered. This drive included the old ranch where during the summer and on holidays I helped my younger brother raise cattle. I also drove by our old home.

As soon as I pulled up in front of the two-story house on Berkley Street I had one of those flashback memories. It was of eating homemade ice cream in the backyard, typically peach, my father's favorite. I remember my mother sending me to the old icehouse to purchase ice for the ice cream freezer. The old icehouse was as authentic as you can get, with a high loading dock, plenty of sawdust, and ice that came in huge blocks. There was one modern feature: mounted next to the huge freezer was a large grinder, and you could get a sack and have the machine chop the ice for you rather than doing it by hand at home. For some reason, ice cream made with that ice always tasted better than with the prebagged ice that one can buy from convenience stores.

You have probably guessed that I've reached the age where sentimentality often trumps common sense. I've been known to say that attic fans provided better cooling at night than air conditioning, and that we were better off before interstate highways bypassed our small towns and villages. I now offer the proclamation that the death of icehouses is one more sign of cultural degeneration.

I confess that I don't fully understand the reason for this, except to point out that we are eating less and less homemade ice cream and more and more of the stuff that claims to be homemade but is bought in a store. We tend to eat it in the kitchen rather than the backyard, and we enjoy it less even though it seems to pack on more pounds than the homemade variety.

My theory is that once things become too easy they lose some of their appeal. Perhaps more importantly, once the rituals are gone—the trip to the icehouse, calling the neighbors over, taking turns on the hand crank—the romance is gone. And if there is anything that we need in our prosaic and consumer-driven world, it is a touch of romance, a bit of poetry, a ritual here and there that reminds us that quality of life cannot be measured by the same standards of efficiency and productivity we have become accustomed to in the business world.

Somewhere in America there is surely a functioning icehouse. If it is within fifty miles of you, I hope you are already planning your next visit. If not, try taking the time to create some new rituals for you and your loved ones. Slow down. Enjoy the journey. Experience the romance.

7 Junk Folder

I do my share of teasing about modern technology, but there is one innovation of the digital age that I wholeheartedly endorse: the junk folder. At least that is what it is called in my e-mail program.

You surely know what it is and how it works. If you receive unwelcome messages that are not caught by a spam program, you can tag that sender and have future messages dumped into the junk folder. You don't have to allow those messages to fill your inbox, nor do you have to take the time to read and delete them. You put them in the junk folder and forget about them.

I forget which president it was (maybe Eisenhower) who had a special drawer for anonymous letters. When he opened a letter he would look for a signature and, if there was none, he would toss the letter into his junk drawer without reading it. Every once in a while the junk drawer was emptied into the trash.

The concept of a junk folder has a powerful meaning in the relationship with God that Jesus calls us into. If you are like me, there are all sorts of messages and memories that fill your brain with guilt, regret, shame, embarrassment, and feelings of failure. Some of those messages are surely justified by genuine failures and sins, and others are probably the residue of someone else's thoughtless comment, or maybe your own sensitivity to an issue of little importance. Either way, God's grace invites us to forgive and forget: forgive yourself because God has, and forget by permanently filing those thoughts, feelings, and memories in the junk folder, never to be opened again.

For the obsessive-compulsive among us (at least half of us are, including yours truly) there is always the tendency to go back and relive the pain. For some reason we feel compelled to retrace the steps of every stupid thing we have ever said or done. If you are one of those, follow these steps: go to the junk folder in your brain, click on "Select All," and then hit the "Delete" button. When you see "These messages will be permanently deleted. Are you sure? Y/N," hit the "Yes" button. Then, listen for this message from God: "Well done, good and faithful servant."

7- The Reunion

One week after I graduated from Denison High School in May of 1966, my family moved back to Dallas. I had been the luckiest of all teenage boys. Having moved to Denison in September of my freshman year, I was able to spend four full school years with the same kids before graduating with them. But it was much more than that. Denison was a rural-themed Disneyland for this city boy. We bought and raised cattle, rode horses, played football, and waterskied all over Lake Texoma. No one could have had more fun during those four years than I.

Nevertheless, after I drove out of town on that June morning of 1966, I never returned. I went off to college and, with no family left in town, I didn't make it back for Thanksgiving,

Christmas, or summer holidays. I think I went to a small Friday night gathering for my tenth reunion, and that was the only time in the past four-and-a-half decades that I've seen most of those classmates with whom I graduated.

All of that changed on a Friday night not long ago when I, with great anxiety and trepidation, returned to Denison for my forty-fifth high school reunion. How could I go back and be with people whom I had not seen in all those years? What would we talk about? What would be the point in trying to close a gap that had grown to almost five decades? I admit I was scared to death. I am quite used to meeting strangers, but how does one meet and converse with strangers he has known for forty-five years?

It was a surreal experience. I felt as if I had been in a time warp because, almost from the moment I walked into the reunion, those forty-five years seemed to melt away, at least in some ways. We all looked different, we all had acquired decades of experience that was different from our shared experience of high school, but almost immediately the camaraderie, the joking and the kidding, and some of the old buffoonery surfaced. For a few hours that Friday night, I wasn't really sure whether I was seventeen or sixty-three, or some weird combination of the two.

Driving back to Plano, I continued to process the event. I told my wife that I was unclear about what that reunion meant for my life. But one thing I learned: We never just drive off and leave the past behind. We never really forget the ones who have been important to us. For better or for worse, we have been formed by all those relationships from years gone by. That discovery was not bittersweet. It was sweet. Really sweet.

To the class of 1966, thanks for welcoming me back home, and for reminding me that you will always, always be a part of my life.

7 · 1948 Studebaker

I was on Parkwood Boulevard when I pulled up behind it: a blue 1948 Studebaker. I almost couldn't believe my eyes. It was in mint condition, and the three occupants looked as if they were going out to dinner or something, as if there was nothing unusual about their mode of transportation. I knew better: this car is a true antique because it was manufactured in the year of my birth. And it is unique because it is, apparently, still working.

I know of a lot of things from 1948 that aren't still working. For instance, my knees are barely functioning. Our youth minister is preparing to run the New York Marathon, whereas I feel pretty good if I am able to walk from the parking lot to my office without the use of anti-inflammatory drugs. That goes for most of the other joints in my body. High school football, years of riding horses, and old age create a toxic combination. I kept staring at the Studebaker with the thought that it must have been gently used all those years.

On the other hand, it seems to me that the goal in life should be to use up all of God's gifts by the time one comes to the end. I forget the details, but I remember seeing a plaque in St. Paul's Cathedral in London that honored a saint from another era. It read, "Like a candle, he burned himself out in service to God." That has always stuck in my mind as a fine tribute to a life well-lived. Lots of athletes like to say before a game, "Let's leave it all on the field." In other words, win or lose, let's not return to the locker room and have any doubts about whether we gave 100 percent effort. That should be true about the game of life itself.

I'm starting to feel better about my knees. Also about my first vehicle, a 1949 pickup truck that we drove until it finally fell apart. I suspect, by comparison, it gave much more value than that 1948 Studebaker. When the time comes to depart, I hope someone will say that I burned the candle to the very end.

7- Blessing Us in Disguise

Not long ago I took a drive down a county road that lies south of Muenster, Texas. It was a road I had never been on before, and it took me into some stunningly beautiful ranch and farm land. I couldn't take my eyes off the pastures and meadows; fortunately there was practically no traffic. It may have been the greenest spring season I had ever seen in north Texas.

The irony was the cold, wet winter everyone complained about a few months before helped create the fantastic spring growing season. I admit it was also accompanied by a world-class allergy season, but that is another subject. What is of interest to me is that, other than the allergies, what appeared a few months before to be bad news had ripened into truly good news. The world was blooming with new life, and we owed it in part to the cold, wet winter.

That is the way it happens much of the time, is it not? Things happen to us that are uncomfortable or upsetting at the time, but when we look back we see that God was blessing us in disguise. So many times we can't see that the failure, or the lost job, or the missed opportunity was really a doorway into a future we could never have anticipated.

Typically, I like to focus on looking forward rather than backward. But I have come to believe that most of us cannot really understand the "faith" thing unless we occasionally glance back to see how God has been working in our lives. When we do, it usually calls for a prayer of thanksgiving, accompanied by a little less anxiety about the road forward. Understanding that God has always been there in the past sure helps when it comes to trusting in God's presence and power for the challenges that lie in the future.

7- The First Time

I was talking to one of our moms on a Monday afternoon about her young daughter. That morning she had taken her to public school for the very first time. She was sharing with me the many and varied emotions both she and her daughter had experienced during that milestone moment.

Many of you have gone through this, and so you know how emotional the experience is. Just listening to her story, I found myself saying that I dread the day that my grandson goes off to school for the first time.

Upon reflection I realized that was not a completely accurate statement. Those first-time experiences generally entail a mixture of emotions that are both painful and pleasurable.

Hopefully the anxiety and dread are balanced by the joy and hope that accompanies the knowledge that your child is growing up and becoming the person God meant him or her to be. I can tell you that I love bringing my grandson to our Children's Discovery Center preschool here at our church because *he* loves it so much. He can't wait to get there on schooldays. Hopefully he will take to public school the same way.

All of this has made me introspective. I have been thinking about the fact that there is still a little boy inside of me that both fears and eagerly anticipates the first time. I will always remember that mixture of emotions I felt when I went off the high diving board the first time; when I took off and piloted an airplane by myself for the first time; when I stood in the pulpit to preach my first sermon. Even though I am now into my seventh decade, that little boy still emerges when I am called to do something for the very first time.

So here is the question for the day: What first-time experiences have you been postponing for no other reason than simple anxiety? Taking a continuing education course of some kind? Visiting a church or Sunday school class? Introducing yourself to someone you'd like to know? I'm preaching to myself as much as you, but here is the bottom line: If your five-year-old can handle it, so can you. In fact, you might even find it to be an exhilarating experience.

7- The Laundry

Coming through the little town of Valentine, Texas, I saw a sight I have not witnessed in years. Behind a little hut of a house, the newly washed laundry was hanging out to dry. It was a perfect day for such activity: dry, sunny, and with a nice little breeze. Even if you are old enough to remember the days before indoor dryers, you will have to admit that there was something unique and humorous about this particular scene: the laundry was hanging on a barbed wire fence!

It brought back memories, of course. I can remember when nearly every house had a clothesline in the backyard. I recall getting into trouble with my mother for running into the newly washed clothes and knocking them down (I think that maybe I did it on purpose—all those flapping garments and sheets were too much temptation for a little boy with excess energy). Best of all, I can remember the special smell of those sun-dried sheets when I got into bed at night. In spite of our modern machines and technology, sheets dried by a machine will never feel and smell as good as those dried outside.

In our modern world it is sometimes difficult to remember what is important and what is not. We get fooled into thinking we can't possibly make it without a new wide-screen television, the latest edition computer game, or a cellular phone. We tend to forget that most of the world doesn't have a clue about many of those things. We take our washers and dryers (old technology) for granted.

Somewhere in west Texas tonight a child will go to bed without an iPod or a PlayStation or any hope of having one in the near future. But their laundry will be clean, and their sheets will smell better than ours. Even without a clothes dryer, life will be good.

7 The Legacy

August 9 was my father's birthday, and I have been thinking about him. He died in 1987 at the age of sixty-one, shattering my illusion that such a life force should live to at least eighty-seven, which is what he would be today. I confess how deeply I wish he had lived to meet his great-grandsons; even more, how I wish his great-grandsons could have the opportunity to meet him and size up the one who left such a great legacy of life and service.

Ironically, I just this morning finished Jon Meacham's book *Franklin and Winston*. It is a riveting account of the friendship of the two men who saved the world from evil. In the telling of the story, Meacham takes his readers by the hand and leads them through a history lesson of World War II. I could not help but remember my father telling about trying to enlist on the day after the attack on Pearl Harbor, December 8, 1941, and being told to come back when he was old enough. One year later he joined the Navy.

Having spent the last couple of days in such close proximity to the Greatest Generation, I have been asking myself: what is the difference between then and now, between them and us? When you read the details of the story, you certainly understand that these "heroes were not pure souls," as Nikos Kazantzakis once said of his own family (*Report to Greco* [Simon and Schuster, 2012], chapter 16). There were secrets and intrigues, outsized ambitions and jealousies, the lust for power. No, these were flawed humans, just as has been the case since creation.

Perhaps it was the conspiracy of history rather than some innate quality of the people, but I believe the defining characteristic of the Greatest Generation was their devotion to a cause far greater than themselves. It was Winston Churchill pleading to the British people, in the darkest moments of the Battle of Britain, that history might one day judge this to have been "their finest hour." It was a farm kid in a foxhole who didn't understand international politics at all, but did understand loyalty to one's comrades. It was the sacrifice of mothers and wives and children who mobilized because they believed in the values that were being defended.

We live in a day when the smallest action or inconsequential statement can set Twitter on fire; when we dissect and analyze every word and syllable; when all it takes to divide us is one misguided word or opinion. We inhabit a world in which political or ideological differences can evidently not be forgotten or forgiven. Oh, how I long for a revival of great ideas and ideals, for a vision that makes us seem small, for a task that unites rather than divides us.

So this is my birthday gift to my father: we will keep trying. Above the discord of our times we can still hear the clarion call to something higher; we still believe in the values of courage and sacrifice; we are still committed to those ideals that unite rather than divide. And so we will keep trying. We owe that to you, the Greatest Generation. And we owe it to your great-grandchildren, the next generation.

7 School

Confession: I was never really big on school. I don't really know the reason for that. I always made excellent grades; I had lots of friends. For some reason, school just seemed like a terrible burden. I can remember being in the first grade and crying in hopes of persuading my parents that I didn't really need to go to school. By the time I got to the fourth grade, stories of Tom Sawyer and Huckleberry Finn had been read to me, and I was convinced that their approach was superior to that of those who believed in mandatory public education.

College and graduate school were different. I loved them, but as I think about it my primary attractions involved noncurricular activities. Looking back, I shudder to think about the number of classes I cut. Even though I still made excellent grades, I can tell you it is only by the grace of God (or perhaps just some understanding professors) that I graduated from the halls of higher education. Come to think about it, it may be just that some of those professors were happy to be rid of me.

Having cleansed myself by means of confession, let me say that the great heroes of today's society are the truly dedicated teachers and administrators who are committed to our children. They not only care about your kindergartner, but they understand that one of the greatest hopes we have for a civil, peaceful, and productive society lies within our common commitment to education. Without a passion for educating our children, America regresses to a time and place that is darker than most of us want to contemplate.

And so here's to school: the mommies and daddies and grandparents who will tearfully but bravely watch as their five-year old begins her journey; all the kids who, either joyfully or reluctantly, will once again leave the parks and swimming pools to return to the daily process of growing smarter and growing up; most of all, the teachers and administrators who have chosen to invest themselves in the most important commodities we produce. To them we say a heartfelt, "Thank you."

7 Mothers

Mary committed these things to memory and considered them carefully. —Luke 2:19 CEB

A couple of years ago I was doing some work up at Siete Ranch and reached for a Bible that was sitting in a bookcase. The Bible had belonged to my mother, and I had never used it before. Upon opening it, I found all sorts of notations and underlining and also various poems and writings stuck in between the pages. But one such insert immediately brought tears. It was an old Christmas gift tag from my younger brother, probably written around age six, and it read: "To Mommy and Daddy. Merry Christmas. Wally."

It had been in that Bible for approximately half a century. I have no idea whether the original gift had been that Bible or something else, but suddenly I had a clear vision of my baby brother, blond-haired and blue-eyed, sitting in his pajamas under the tree expectantly waiting for "Mommy and Daddy" to open his package that had been wrapped and given with boyish enthusiasm.

The strongest emotion came as I thought about all those years that my mother had opened her Bible and found that tag, remembering that Christmas of long ago and pondering in her heart the miraculous gift of children. It was in that moment that

I understood the meaning and power of this particular verse in Luke's story, and perhaps as much as I will ever understand about the particular burden and blessing of being a mother. Luke tells us that Mary "committed" the words of the shepherds "to memory" and "considered them carefully." Surely, like all mothers, she was wondering what would become of this remarkable gift from God that she now cradled to her breast.

Sooner or later all mothers make the painful journey that Mary made: they slowly let go of those precious beings whom they once held so closely and protectively. They somehow find the courage to allow their children to grow up, trusting them completely to the God who brought them into the world as such vulnerable and tiny beings. But I don't think they ever stop "pondering" the meaning of their children, or the miracle of life, or the extraordinary privilege of being chosen by God for what is simultaneously the most joyful and painful of all vocations.

7- Disconnecting

I'm glad to report that I still learn something new every day. Learning new stuff is what makes life adventuresome, and it also keeps us young. For instance, sometime ago I learned that if you accidentally drop a BlackBerry into a glass of iced tea, there is a noticeable decrease in functionality. This was a revelation for me because, up until then, I had never done it before.

I retrieved it quickly, and I was hoping for the best. Sure

enough, I was able to make a phone call, and the quality was excellent. The problem was that I was not able to disconnect from the call. No matter how many times I hit, banged, or cursed the End button, I couldn't get rid of the call. That was just one of a number of technical glitches that I encountered after the accidental drowning of my phone. I couldn't help but think about the years of research that went into telephone technology trying to get a connection, and here I was trying my hardest to disconnect. Alexander Graham Bell must have been rolling over in his grave!

I've heard of cowboys who roped bulls or wild steers when they were "tied on hard and fast" and then regretted doing it because they couldn't disconnect. It can be a pretty daunting experience to be on a thousand-pound horse getting dragged around by a fifteen-hundred-pound bull. That's one of the reasons you will often see cowboys carrying very sharp knives in easily reachable places. Sometimes the ability to disconnect can be a matter of life and death.

I have known people who had difficulty disconnecting from a toxic relationship or an addiction to some drug or activity. In fact, being unable to disconnect may be one of the most common demons that we face while on our very human journeys. I've even known some people who have trouble disconnecting from their job or profession. They carry smart phones with them around the clock, even when on vacation or a day off, so they are never very far from the office.

Uh-oh...do you think that iced tea incident might have been a message from God?

7 "No Noise on My Fingers"

I was taking my three-year-old grandson to vacation Bible school when he asked me to turn on the radio. He loves music, and so I turned to my favorite bluegrass station. To encourage him, I started snapping my fingers. From the extended cab I heard this little voice saying, "DD, I don't have any noise on my fingers."

As an amateur writer I wish I had the creative ability to say things as brilliantly as little children. I can't imagine a better way of expressing the frustration of not yet knowing how to do something. Children have a way of seeing the world and its inhabitants in such a literal way that they sometimes capture the magic/pathos/tragedy of the creation more eloquently than someone such as Shakespeare or Faulkner could have ever dreamed.

A good friend shared with me earlier this week about how his young daughter wrote a note to her great-grandmother after the death of her ninety-seven-year-old husband. Young Mary, having dealt with the death of her dog Nisha last summer, told her that she was sorry her husband was now living with God, but she hoped he might meet some new people and animals in heaven. I don't think that Saint Peter at his best could have written a more eloquent or touching note of condolence.

When I start getting discouraged, I make a point of just spending some time around young children. They see things exactly as they are and describe them in God-language that for some reason has dropped out of the lexicon of us adults. If you listen to them carefully they will describe both the joy and the tragedy of our journeys on earth in a way that will inevitably bring you a little bit closer to God.

7- In the Company of Men

He wore three badges during his career: one as a Texas Ranger, one as a Dallas County Deputy Sheriff, and one as a special investigator for the District Attorney. My mother and uncle called him Daddy, but everyone else in the world, including his grandchildren, called him Bert.

He wore a suit and tie his entire career, but his refined clothes could not disguise the tough interior. I cannot tell you how many times I saw him put his Smith and Wesson on top of the chest of drawers before going to bed. Other than that, it was always discreetly hidden under his suit coat, and everyone knew that this was a man who had arrested Clyde Barrow and sent him to prison in 1930.

Though I was only in grade school, he would often take me to the various places that were a part of his life. I remember going to the old Dallas County Jail where I met other deputies and the legendary sheriff Bill Decker. I recall going back with him to where the cells were and talking with prisoners through the bars. They all seemed to be fond of Bert even though he had brought many of them up there in handcuffs.

Sometimes he would take me late in the night to White Rock Lake where we would visit with friends of his who ran trotlines all night long. There would be campfires, the soft whispers of men who knew each other well, the smell of fish, and the occasional whiff of bourbon. I watched and listened, somehow aware of the fact that I had been invited for a few moments into a rare and mostly exclusive fraternity.

One of my favorite places to go with Bert was to church. Whenever the doors of the old Owenwood Methodist Church were open, Mama and Bert were there. I would stand with them in the pews, singing the old hymns, aware that even in that sacred place Bert's weapon was only inches from my shoulder. I knew that there were men who had threatened to kill him when they got out of prison, but I was never afraid.

My favorite time was before and after church. Bert would take me to stand with him and the other men outside on the large concrete front porch of the sanctuary where they smoked unfiltered cigarettes and talked about politics or the drought. These were hard men, products of the 1920s and 1930s, and I enjoyed being with them.

One of the great myths of the modern church is that it is primarily for women and children. I know better. I always have.

Chapter 4

Nature

I have always loved being outdoors. My childhood memories revolve around endless games of sandlot baseball and football, playing in White Rock Creek that ran behind our house, and the sheer joy of visiting my grandparents' farm in Tennessee.

Through the years I have spent many hours fishing and hunting. Even then I understood that the greatest reward was the joy of being outside, oftentimes with my dog or cherished companions. And when it had been a productive day, there was nothing better than frying the fish over an open campfire.

These days I have come to understand that nature is one of my greatest teachers. I am a constant observer of sunrises and sunsets, of stars, and of the ever-changing weather. On my drives back and forth from Siete Ranch, I am drawn to the beauty of the farmer's field, the enduring faith of the farmer himself, the occasional circling of the red-tailed hawk, the rhythm of the seasons, and the grace of a God that I cannot comprehend but can observe in the wonders of his creation.

If it were in my power I would take every reader for a horseback ride in my beloved Davis Mountains or on a midnight visit to the famed McDonald's Observatory where one can see more stars than can possibly be imagined. I would share pictures of the newborn Hereford calf or sit quietly with you on the front porch of Siete Ranch as the sun goes down. As it is, I offer a few humble thoughts on nature, both fearsome and comforting, but always my great teacher.

7 Serenity

Driving back to Plano from Siete Ranch very early in the morning, I take time to reflect on the sights and sounds of the day. For me, there is nothing comparable to a horse barn just before daybreak: the nickering of the horses as they anticipate the scoop of oats that is coming their way, the smell of hay, and that unique, sweaty smell that emanates only from horses. Sometimes when I rub my mare's forehead we both recall those past moments of perfect unity, those rare and magical times when horse and rider became one.

The eastern horizon is still mostly dark, but there is just enough light to illuminate the dividing line between land and sky. It's enough to promise the beginning of a new day. As I step into the truck to begin my trip to the office, I notice a wisp of smoke rising from the dying embers of the fire pit from last night's cookout, and warm memories return of trusted friends and lively conversation.

As I'm driving south on FM 1385, the sun begins to peek over the horizon and lights up the green wheat that has somehow miraculously sprung from the dark earth. Only two weeks ago, I drove by the farmer who was planting in the midst of drought, and I marveled at the simple faith of those who till the land. This morning I marvel at the abundant grace of the one who waters the earth and grows the crop.

In the midst of this comes a sense of tremendous thanksgiving for the gift of another day. Life is not perfect. I face challenges, including some minor ones and one or two huge ones. I have lingering sadness over the accumulating losses of family and friends that come inevitably to anyone who has entered his seventh decade. But nevertheless, on this morning, I am moved by an overwhelming gratitude for all that has been and all that is. I contemplate the amazing truth that I wouldn't trade places with anyone.

It does not happen nearly enough for me, but I cannot help thinking that this moment is what the good life is supposed to be at its best: absolute gratitude for all that I have rather than all that I want. I turn east on Highway 380, headed for the office and a busy day, but with the grace-filled knowledge that I have experienced one of those extraordinary moments that can only be described as serenity.

7- The Mesquite Tree

When I was in college my brothers and I leased a big pasture in Wichita Falls for the purpose of raising cattle. It was full of mesquite trees. When we would get on our horses to round up the cows, it was truly an ordeal. Those cows would hide in those thick mesquites and as soon as you ran them out from one, they would go back behind another. Not to mention that running into the thorns on a mesquite is like getting stuck by an ice pick. Our horses didn't appreciate it any better than we did.

It is my understanding that mesquites were carried into Texas several centuries ago by Catholic priests intent on evangelizing the Indians. I don't remember the exact story about how it occurred, but surely it was an accident as I am convinced that no God-fearing man would purposely bring such a vile plant onto such sacred land (pardon the Texas pride).

I have never been a fan of the mesquite tree. However, as I passed a thick grove of them on the side of the highway not too long ago, I was prompted to rethink my lifelong belief that there is no use under the sun for such a plant. For some reason I started thinking about food and the hundreds of steaks I have cooked over an open fire through the years. I have used every conceivable fuel (propane gas being by' far the least desirable) including oak, hickory, cherry, walnut, and pecan. This you can take to the bank: there is no better way to cook a steak than over mesquite coals. Hickory or pecan is better for smoking a brisket or ribs, but mesquite was made for steaks.

Maybe it is true that God has a reason and a purpose for everything under the sun. On balance, I'm not sure if the virtues of the mesquite tree outweigh its vices or not, but this I do know: there are certain nights when the embers of my mesquite fire offset the dying light of the setting sun, the sweet smell of grease hitting those mesquite coals wafts through the air, the steaks sizzle, and I give thanks for ancient monks who trudged through this rugged country bringing religion and mesquite.

7- Simple Faith

In the fall a few years ago, during one of Texas's worst droughts, I passed a farmer who was running a harrow over a plowed field, evidently preparing it for planting a crop of winter wheat. The ground was parched, and the dust rose from the harrow like talcum powder. The nearby stock tanks were dried up, and the ground was riddled with cracks that appeared to run all the way to China. Nevertheless, the farmer was preparing the ground in anticipation of dropping the precious seeds into the soil.

I found that to be a remarkably inspiring sight. Jesus often used agricultural examples when talking about faith. And what could be more faithful than a farmer sowing seed in the midst of the worst drought since the 1950s?

Agricultural consultants estimated it would take twelve to fifteen inches of rain in order to heal the land enough to make it productive again, and the meteorological experts predicted another long winter of La Niña, which means warmer and dryer than usual. But this farmer was acting on the faith that, sooner or later, it will rain. Sooner or later the land will again blossom with the dark green color of growing wheat.

Have you been through a dry spell recently? At work? In your marriage? Trouble with your kids or with finances? I wonder what it would mean to exercise the simple faith of a farmer.

Jesus was so right when he told us about the faith of those who plant the crop. It is, perhaps, our strongest metaphor for what it means to live faithfully in times of doubt or trouble or malaise. Today my prayer is a simple one: "Lord, give me the simple faith of those who till the ground for a living. Amen."

7- The Mustard Seed

"I assure you that if you have faith the size of a mustard seed, you could say to this mountain, 'Go from here to

there,' and it will go. There will be nothing that you can't do."
—Matthew 17:20 CEB

The recent closing of the Space Shuttle program by NASA prompted me to pause for a few minutes in front of a framed note that sits in an anteroom to my office. It was given to my father over three decades ago, and my father gave it to me. The note has a tiny mustard seed glued to it, and below are these handwritten words:

"This mustard seed was flown to the moon aboard Apollo 16.

"With Best Wishes, Charlie Duke, LMP." (Lunar Module Pilot)

There is, of course, more to the story. The mustard seed was one of several given to Charles Duke by Norman Vincent Peale, and it refers to the text cited above. Dr. Peale wanted to fly the gospel to the moon and back, and he chose the mustard seed as the symbol of that mission.

Every now and then I stare at this little memento. I understand why Jesus chose the mustard seed for his statement because it is extraordinarily small and inconspicuous. You wouldn't think it could accomplish much at all, but a mustard tree can grow to be huge, with large branches and abundant shade. Jesus was saying that a little bit of faith can yield enormous results.

I think about the faith of those early space pioneers who *believed* that humans would one day walk on the moon. Do you think it would have ever happened if there hadn't been someone who dreamed it and believed it? Do you think the Wright brothers would have ever "broken the bonds of earth" if they had not had faith that it could be done? What is it in your life that is being held back because you don't have enough faith?

There is an interesting postscript to this Apollo 16 story. After returning from space, Charles Duke gave his life to Christ and commenced a very active life as a Christian layperson. You might have thought that, after accomplishing something so remarkable, he would have come back convinced of the greatness of the human being. Instead, he returned from the moon convinced of the reality and magnificence of God. Dr. Peale must have known what he was doing when he asked Charlie Duke to fly those tiny little symbols of faith to the moon.

7 Hot!

I remember crossing the state line into Texas one late afternoon during the great drought of the 1950s. It was July or August, and we were coming through Texarkana in a 1953 Oldsmobile with no air-conditioning. All the windows were down, and wind was blowing through as if heated by a blow torch. Three boys were squeezed together in the back seat. As we crossed the state line we noticed a temperature gauge at a filling station that read 110 degrees.

It had been our custom to sing "The Eyes of Texas" as we crossed the state line. My father, a native Tennessean with a good voice, would lead this little production, and so he did on this occasion. We did our best, but I have to say that, on that particular day, our hearts weren't really in it.

If you grew up in Texas during the 1950s as I did, you

perhaps share with me a mild paranoia about someday returning to another drought lasting nearly a decade. It decimated the farming and ranching families of our state, and since agriculture drove much of the Texas economy in those days, the pain was felt by all. I can remember seeing White Rock Lake in Dallas when it wasn't much larger than a swimming pool. It helped me understand everything I was hearing from the grownups.

When I wrote this we were two months into one of the worst heat/drought spells since the 1950s. As an owner of cows and buyer of hay, it had me more existentially concerned than when I was a child. This is how it works: when there is no rain there is no pasture, and there is no hay. When there is no hay the only alternative is to sell cows. When everyone is selling cows because there is no hay, there is no big paycheck when you leave the sale barn. Such is the angst that comes with being a cattleman, whether large or small.

It is easier for me to say this than many whose livelihoods, rather than avocations, depend on the cattle business. Nevertheless, it is true. There is a rhythm to life that lies beyond the understanding of mere mortals. When will it rain next? When will the temperatures drop? It is not ours to know. But, sooner or later, the temperatures will drop, the rain will come, the earth will turn green. Such is the rhythm of nature. Such is the nature of life.

7 Well Water

If you've ever worked outside in really hot, dry, dusty conditions, you perhaps have known the joy of well water. While the taste of well water varies, the feel of well water is pretty consistent, and it is the feeling of really cold water in the summertime that I enjoy.

I remember as a boy drawing water from the well at my grandfather's farm and pouring it into a porcelain bowl in order to wash up. The bowl, a towel, and a small dish with soap on it stood on a wash stand, and the kids all stood in line for their turn to wash in that ice cold water. We all enjoyed this ritual of washing in the same way our Underwood and Kelly predecessors had done for generations. Sometime in the future I will share with you the details of what came next, which was dinner on the screened-in back porch.

We don't have our own well at Siete Ranch, but we enjoy the water that comes out of deep wells that are a part of a local water cooperative. I've done some of that hot, dry, dusty work in recent weeks, and one of the compensations is going into the house and turning on the tap to receive that ice cold water on my hands, arms, and face.

There is a story in the Bible about a woman who was drawing water from Jacob's well when Jesus asked her for a drink. She was there at noon, and it must have been hot and dry. Jesus and the disciples were surely thirsty, and I know they were glad to be at this deep well of their ancestor where they could enjoy that which is the gift of life. It is interesting to me that Jesus, in his conversation with this woman, compares God's grace with "living water" (John 4:11) from a well so deep that it never runs dry.

I think that sometime in the next fifty years, water in Texas may become almost as scarce and precious as it was in the time of Jesus. Today we take it for granted, but to our peril. Without water, there is no life. That thought brings real appreciation as I dip my hands into the well water at Siete Ranch, and it deepens my understanding of how our relationship with God is truly the gift of life.

7 The Wheat Harvest

Driving south on FM 1385 after dark, I saw headlights in front of me, on the east side of the road, their light filtered through the dust and the darkness of the night. Soon I heard the drumming of the big combine engines and saw the eighteen-wheel trucks lined up on the caliche road bordering the north part of the field, waiting to be filled. I closed the windows of my truck as I approached the huge cloud of dust billowing onto the highway.

This wheat field, which I have watched for many months now as it matured from tiny green stalks to "amber waves of grain," was finally being harvested. This may sound silly to some, but it was a thrilling moment for me, even as I gagged a bit on the distinct-tasting wheat dust that had already invaded the air inside my pickup. I could not help but think of the power of this tradition. Year after year, decade after decade, century after century, the harvest has been the culmination of a year's worth of planning and hard work.

My only sadness came in the recognition, once again, that the family farm is nearly a relic of the past. That thought provoked powerful childhood memories of Underwood relatives, dressed in overalls and standing by a tractor, smoking hand-rolled cigarettes and discussing the weather. These were men who had first tilled that west Tennessee soil with mules and single-bottom plows, who still drew their bath water from wells, and who remembered when the Tennessee Valley Authority first turned on the switch that brought electricity to their rural farms. These are memories that grow stronger with age, and I wonder how I can pass them on to my grandsons.

Tomorrow morning when you butter your toast at breakfast, eat your sandwich at noon, or indulge in a piece of cake in the evening, take a moment to give thanks for the wheat harvest, the farmers, the combine operators, the truck drivers, and all those who participate in this age-old ritual of helping to put bread upon our tables. Whether you know it or not, you carry within you the genes of ancient relatives whose entire lives revolved around the simple but profound traditions of the wheat harvest.

7 Cold Front

Sitting at my desk on a Thursday morning at Siete Ranch, I check the weather map on my computer. It confirms that the leading edge of an approaching cold front lies just a few miles to the west, and that it is moving slowly my way. Earlier, as I was unsaddling my mare, a few gusts of wind from what meteorologists call the outflow boundary had already alerted me to the storm's pending arrival. Soon, the much coveted rain will begin.

This particular cold front promises to bring the greatly needed wet stuff, but not the dangerous weather often associated with these kinds of fronts. Anyone who lives in north Texas can testify to the terrifying disruption that often accompanies this kind of weather. Thunderstorms, lightning strikes, high straight-line winds, and the occasional twister are known accomplices when this kind of frontal boundary approaches. In winter, they sometimes arrive embedded in bitterly cold temperatures.

Years of watching and living through this kind of weather has taught me some valuable lessons. I guess they could be summed up by saying that one learns to take the bad along with the good and to anticipate the remarkable peacefulness that inevitably follows. In this case, the skies will clear in a few days, blanketing us with that gorgeous azure color that remains when a north wind has cleared out the haze and smog. The humidity will drop, but the grass will begin to grow, leaving us with creation at its best.

I am always astonished when I think about the parallels between the natural world and our own imperfect lives. It doesn't make a difference who you are—how talented, smart, or successful you might be—the storms always arrive. They come in various disguises—illness, financial problems, broken love affairs—and the leading edge of these storms always looks more threatening than promising. They disrupt our lives in one way or another. But this much you can take to the bank: they always pass, and when they do, they leave us in a state of grace. If we have been listening to God, we discover the remarkable truth that we have, to paraphrase author William Faulkner, not only survived but prevailed.

The older I grow the more convinced I become that God blesses our lives by disrupting them.

7 Rain

The Bible says that it rains on the just and unjust alike. True as that is, my neighbors seem to get rain when I do not.

I know this sounds like whining, but two nights ago I watched the radar for a couple of hours. It was pure joy as I watched the kaleidoscopic green, yellow, and red colors hover over Siete Ranch. My mind filled with visions of green grass and fat cows. Last night I learned the bitter truth: one-half inch of the precious wet stuff was all I got. After a severe two-month drought, that was merely enough to wet the parched lips of my thirsty ground.

What I am about to share here is the best wisdom I have to offer after over sixty years on this earth. I was thrilled with my half-inch. It was not always that way. I used to get really frustrated that two inches fell on my neighbor to the west, and three inches on the farmers to the north, while Siete Ranch remained relatively dry. It just didn't seem fair.

I now understand—sort of—that fairness has nothing to do with it. As it says in Job, where was I when God created the heavens and earth? The message has been sent, loud and clear, that the irrigation system belongs to God and not me.

I know full well that most of you aren't obsessed with rain in the same way I am. I didn't worry about rain all that much until Siete Ranch came into my life. But what we do share in common is our struggle with the blessings and challenges. As a pastor I have observed this for years: one family seems to receive showers of blessings while another struggles with one tragedy or challenge after another. Why is that? As I have often said from the pulpit, if I am ever lucky enough to get to the Pearly Gates, I have lots of questions for which I would like answers.

As I enter the final chapter of my life (which I hope will be a very long one), I am becoming a bit more sanguine about all of these issues. Railing against the apparent injustices of life has no usefulness whatsoever and only produces frustration and an ill temper. The whole reason that faith is important to us is that living the good life means trusting to God all those things over which we have no control.

And so I hereby correct a statement I made earlier: God did not send a half-inch of rain to the parched lips of *my* thirsty ground. The blessed land of Siete Ranch, and all that is above and below it, belongs to God, not me. I am the luckiest person in the world because I have been granted stewardship of it for a short spell, and I am much better off when I remember that. The same is true of my very life and the blessings of family, friends, and meaningful work that have been granted to me.

I have noticed that the forecast for the remainder of the week calls for a good chance of rain. I hope to get some, but more than that I pray that I might receive and practice the faith of the old fathers and mothers of the desert. I am speaking here of the great ones of the Old Testament who passed it on from one generation to the next. When it rains or when it doesn't, may I say, "Blessed be the name of the LORD." In the daylight hours or in the darkness may I say, "Blessed be the name of the LORD." In times of birth or in times of earthly death, may I say, "Blessed be the name of the LORD" (Job 1:21 KJV).

7 BlackBerry Heaven

Ever since I was convinced to get a handheld device I have been in BlackBerry Hell. This little computer that fits in my shirt pocket is not only a phone, but receives all my e-mail, keeps my calendar, receives text messages, and stores the numbers and e-mail addresses for over seven hundred contacts.

Being the compulsive personality that I am, I have been tethered to the thing for the last eight months, and it has begun to feel very much like the proverbial tiger by the tail. Whether walking, driving, or riding a horse, I have it with me. As my workout buddies will testify, I keep it with me and often use it at 6:30 in the morning while on the elliptical trainer. It beeps for e-mails (forty to fifty a day), it rings for phone calls, and it makes this weird sound for text messages. From the moment I awaken till I go to bed, it is my constant companion.

Well, something good happened last week. I spent seven days in a cabin with no air-conditioning other than the breezes provided by open windows with no screens. Before you start feeling sorry for me, let me add that I was in the Davis Mountains of far west Texas, and I slept under three blankets in order to keep warm at night. I ate three good meals every day, all of them prepared by cowboy cooks who know how to prepare *cabrito*, chili macho, homemade biscuits, and cherry cobbler using the coals of open wood fires, and all of them consumed in the open with the smell of those fires perfuming the air around me. And . . . with limited cell phone service, I started leaving my BlackBerry in my cabin.

I hate to hype this too much, but it was pretty much a

life-changing moment for me. I had forgotten what life without cell phones is like. Let me tell you, it is pretty good. I finally decided that staff members could go a few days without my input, that I could catch up with e-mail after vacation (it took a few hours, but I got it done in one sitting), and that I didn't need to check on the stock market or news every few hours. I was in BlackBerry Heaven, which means that the handheld device and I were in different locations.

7- Disastrous Christmas

Forty years ago I was the youth minister at a church in a county seat town. There was a strong tradition in this church of providing a live nativity scene every year, and it was the responsibility of the youth minister to somehow pull this off. I later figured out why no truly sane person would accept this assignment for more than a few years in a row, so it was a natural match for the youth minister, who rarely lasts more than a few years at best.

When I say this was a live nativity scene, I am talking about every part. We had live people, a live donkey, some live sheep, everything but a camel. And, of course, it was the animals that caused all the problems. Well, the animals and the occasional adult who would show up to play Joseph in a state that could be described as less than stone sober.

During the three years I oversaw this production, everything that could happen did. The donkey jumped out of the trailer on the way to the church one night and had to be roped on its romp down Main Street. One of the sheep got loose and ran over the baby Jesus, prompting Joseph to utter a word not found in the original text. The Wise Men accidentally knelt in a spot that had been thoroughly fertilized by the creatures, giving rise to quite vocal speculation among the onlookers about how wise men could be that dumb.

Looking back on my years as the director of this fiasco, my fondest memories are of all the things that went wrong. Frankly, we knew each year that something would go horribly awry, and it was that knowledge that caused us to enter into the annual venture with such high morale and anticipation. It would have been no fun whatsoever had the animals cooperated, or had the actors acted professionally. It was the unknown but inevitable and looming disaster that lent real color to this event, and once it was over each year we all began the ritual of saying "never again" while secretly pondering whether next year's catastrophe could possibly outdo this one.

If you are aware of my fondness for analogy and think I am describing your Christmas experience, you are only half right. When you read the actual text, you discover that the original Christmas was a strange mixture of disaster and joy, of plans laid and plans disrupted, of people at their best and people at their worst. That's the way Christmas has been happening for two thousand years now. I think it must be God's way of blessing the messiness of our ordinary lives.

7 Don't Miss the Diversions

I wrote this entry late on a Wednesday evening after a thirty-six-hour turnaround flight to Nashville, Tennessee.

Nashville has been a regular travel destination for me for the past eight or nine years. It is home to several of our denominational agencies, and I go there fairly often.

As I sat down on the plane on Tuesday the person sitting next to me asked if I live in Nashville. When I said no, she asked if I was going to the Grand Ole Opry. I told her no, that it was a business trip, but her question got me to thinking.

I went to the Grand Ole Opry a few months ago because those who planned the meeting I attended made it a part of the agenda after a long day of work. But it was the only time I have ever been. Had they not planned it, I would not have gone. If there are any other tourist destinations in Nashville, I don't know about them. I fly there, go to meetings, and then come home.

I wonder how many of us live our daily lives that way. We move from one place to the other, one task to the next, focused on the business at hand, and fail to enjoy the diversions of life, which are plentiful. And you don't have to go to Nashville or Hawaii to enjoy them.

Recently I took a walk near my home and saw houses that I had never noticed and beautiful landscaping that I pass every day without enjoying. I even took time to watch part of a track meet at the nearby school. It was a great hour I spent just taking in the attractions of my own neighborhood.

What about you? What kind of beauty or humor or excitement do you miss on a daily basis because you are so focused on business or work? How many exciting cities have you traveled to without taking in the history or the beauty? What about the sights in your own neighborhood that you consistently miss because you aren't looking?

It's not too late to change. Now might be a great time to commit to the idea of taking everything in. Sometimes God hides the best gifts right next to us.

7 The Gashouse Gang

I grew up hearing about the Gashouse Gang. It was only natural. My father was from Tennessee, and the nearest professional baseball franchise was the St. Louis Cardinals. Growing up in the 1930s and 1940s, before the days of television, meant that most people followed and became fans of the team that they could most easily listen to on the radio. In Tennessee that was St. Louis, and so my father, uncle, and cousins were all Cardinal fans. That's how I learned about the Gashouse Gang.

The 1934 Cardinals were, arguably, the most colorful team in the history of baseball. Not only did they beat the powerful Detroit Tigers in the World Series, but their roster contained the names of some of the flashiest players to ever put on the uniform: Leo "the Lip" Durocher, Pepper Martin, "Wild Bill" Hallahan, and the Dean brothers, Dizzy and Daffy. My generation, of course, grew up hearing Dizzy Dean, surely the most colorful baseball announcer ever.

A recent newspaper article in the *Dallas Morning News* described the team well with this quotation from a newly published book: they were "a squad of quarreling, slovenly, brilliant misfits...the unique product of a particular time and place" (John Heidenry, *The Gashouse Gang* [New York: Public Affairs, 2008], ix). They were, in other words, the perfect team for the Great Depression of the 1930s.

Here is what I learned from that same article: they were brought together by a "nonimbibing Methodist who would not even watch them play on a Sunday because his religious principles forbade it" (ibid). That man's name was Branch Rickey. Later, with the Brooklyn Dodgers, Branch Rickey would do one of the most courageous things in the history of sports. He broke the color barrier and hired Jackie Robinson, and the game has never been the same. And can there be any doubt that it was his Methodist "principles" that led him to risk everything, including his reputation, for the sake of justice?

7 Coat Hangers

Okay, this is what happened. I decided to clean out my closet. I had been working on a sermon about the importance of caring for the earth. Part of that sermon dealt with consumption and the opportunities we have to live more simply. I walked into my closet, took one look, and decided to practice what I preach by giving to charity every piece of clothing that I had not worn in the past year.

It was a powerful experience. I had collected all of this stuff I no longer use. I began to visualize how nice it would be to have a simple wardrobe of nice clothes I wear rather than a closet stuffed to overflowing with garments I never wear. I began to pull down armloads of shirts, jeans, and jackets. But in the process I kept finding dozens of empty coat hangers. Where did they all come from?

Have you ever noticed how subtle coat hangers are about

their breeding activities? The coat hangers in my closet had been multiplying quickly and silently for years. You're not going to believe this, but I created over three linear feet of extra space on the closet rods by just getting rid of the unused coat hangers.

Additionally, I probably created another four or five linear feet of rod space with the clothes that I took to give to charity. Perhaps more important, I created some space in my life by taking into account and affirming what it is that I reasonably need in terms of clothes. I also eliminated an enormous amount of clutter that I was confronting every morning. It was a liberating experience.

I've been thinking about other ways that we can simplify life. I wonder about the unnecessary baggage that we all carry around: bad memories, guilt, others whom we have not forgiven, anxiety about those things over which we have no control—need I go on? The more I think about it the more it seems that they are the coat hangers of our spiritual lives. They have a tendency to silently multiply and take up enormous emotional and spiritual space, and yet they serve no purpose.

Do we really need all those coat hangers? I don't think so. Getting rid of them not only simplifies life, but can be the first step to empowering us for a much richer way of living.

7- Small Things Make a Difference

I remember hearing my father talk about the great flood of the 1930s in one of the towns he lived in as a child. I have forgotten exactly which town it was in Tennessee or Kentucky, nor do I remember the name of the river that overflowed its banks, but I recall vividly my father's description of seeing people hanging onto their rooftops in the midst of the deluge.

I also remember the drought of the 1950s here in Dallas and how they said it would take years to fill the newly created Lake Dallas. But the drought was broken by an incredibly rainy season, and the newly formed lake was overflowing within a few months. All it took was a little rain.

One Monday I awakened at 5:45 AM and, as is my habit, turned on my computer. Before I looked at my e-mail, I glanced at the weather radar and saw that there were huge storms dumping an astonishing amount of rain on the Lake Kiowa and Collinsville area. Siete Ranch being halfway between Lake Kiowa and Collinsville, it was in the eye of the storm. I dressed quickly, canceled an important trip to Arkansas, and headed north.

To make a long story short, it would be twelve hours before the floodwaters receded enough for me to even get to Siete, and even then I had to make an extra forty-mile loop in order to approach from the northwest rather than the southeast. Needless to say, after viewing the devastation along the way, I was grateful and relieved to find horses, cows, and property in reasonably good shape.

What was the cause of so much distress and destruction? Raindrops. Simple, ordinary drops of rain. Lots of them to be sure. But there was no hurricane such as Katrina, no tornado, no earthquake. Just raindrops. Enough of them that they turned the countryside upside down, took lives, destroyed houses and farms and equipment. On the positive side of the ledger is the fact that the lakes are finally filled, the drought is hopefully over, and the land is flowing with water. Lesson learned: even something as small as a drop of rain can make a huge difference when there are lots of them.

I wonder what might happen if the millions of believers in the world were to decide to love God and serve their neighbor with small acts of kindness all at once? No doubt about it, it would be a huge deluge of love. It might even be the beginning of the new Kingdom on earth. Small things really do make a difference.

7 And the Lights Went Out

One Sunday morning at the 10:00 AM service a rather remarkable thing happened: the lights went out. Not just the lights, but the entire power system, including air-conditioning and sound system. It happened just as our associate was concluding the pastoral prayer, and the impact was powerful. There we were, praying in the dark, and the absence of noises as she finished her prayer was astounding. There was a remarkable sense of community and togetherness as we huddled together in the dark.

I have always sincerely believed that the Holy Spirit is present in worship, and that one should go with whatever happens. Especially since I had just concluded a sermon about the Spirit's guidance in our lives, the power failure seemed to be serendipitous. Therefore, I walked into the aisle and used those moments to help us hear and experience what might be the message in that event.

No, what happened wasn't planned, as many people thought. Even in my wildest and most creative moment, I have not considered blacking out several city blocks in order to make a point. Frankly, there is no way that we could have planned a moment as effective as that. It was God's gift to us and we made the most of it.

It seems to me that oftentimes God presents us with dark moments, and that we have the opportunity to resent them or to claim them as God's gifts. Certainly, the failure of our lights doesn't compare to the loss of a loved one, the diagnosis of a terrible disease, or the disintegration of a relationship, but I do believe that in all of those events there is a gift from God. There is something to experience and something to learn.

I have learned we can practice faithfulness by being sensitive to how bad luck or bad news offers us an opportunity to hear a new word from God.

7- Grand Canyon

After driving through the entrance gate to the South Rim of the Grand Canyon, the first opportunity one has to look at this remarkable bit of nature is called Mather's Point. This is not the best view of the canyon, but our eagerness got the best of us. We pulled our car through the full parking lot, exited, and found a place to park along the road. There were dozens of cars, and as we climbed up the shallow embankment that would allow us to stand on the rim, I could see there were perhaps a hundred people already there. As we approached the edge, I knew instinctively that there was something wrong, something out of sync.

It took only a moment for me to figure it out. Here I was, standing in the midst of a huge crowd of people from many nations at one of the world's greatest tourist attractions, and there were no sounds. No human sounds, at least. We were immersed in a kind of eerie silence. Occasionally one could hear the whistling of the wind through the canyon or the clicking of a camera shutter, but that was all. We stood like worshipers offering silent prayers, and the silence was all but overwhelming. It was an unforgettable moment.

It has been said the Grand Canyon has no need of us, but that we need the Grand Canyon. We need it as a reminder of our mortality and of the finiteness of our shadows against those which have been cast by God and time. We need it as a reminder of the spiritual essence of that which is created by God, especially in a world so obsessed by what is temporary and of little value. We need the Grand Canyon as a reminder of that which is large and noble and mystical and beyond words.

We are told in Exodus that when Moses confronted the burning bush, he turned his head in reverence because he knew that he was looking at the face of God. Under the circumstances, it was impossible for us mere mortals to turn away from this magnificent sight. But surely it was more than appropriate that we stand there in worshipful silence as we tried to comprehend this natural wonder that was as close as we had ever been to seeing the face of God.

7 A Really Big God

I wonder if you saw the news article about the activity of a black hole that has been discovered by European astronomers. It seems that the black hole at the center of galaxy NGC 4845 has "awakened" and is "eating" a planet that is 30 times the mass of Jupiter. One news release put it this way: "a planet—or perhaps a brown dwarf star—which strayed too close was swallowed up by the intense gravitational pull of the black hole" ("Slumbering Black Hole Eats Planet 30 Times Mass of Jupiter," *The Huffington Post*, March 4, 2013).

The part of this report that was most interesting to me was the issue of scale. For instance, the galaxy is located 47 million light years from earth, and the black hole has a mass that is 300,000 times that of our sun. I assume that astrophysicists and others can get their minds around those numbers, but I cannot.

The theological history of the church is that we have consistently made God too small and ourselves too important. In the sixteenth century, a Herculean effort on the part of scientists was required to overcome the church's objections to the observable fact that the earth revolves around the sun rather than the other way around. Unfortunately, there have always been those in the church who resist scientific discoveries that demonstrate that God is much bigger than we thought.

The downside of a God large enough to create the universe is that we can't explain everything. We have to acknowledge that there is perhaps more about God that we don't know than we do know. We are required to give up the presumption that we can truly understand God or God's creation or even God's will. We have to embrace mystery.

This concession to humility is not easy to come by, especially among preachers, most of whom suffer from the occupational hazard of occasionally confusing themselves with the Creator. But during the Easter season I like to take a moment to celebrate rather than rue the fact that God is bigger than we thought. I can neither understand nor explain the resurrection, but I embrace it and try to live joyously in the midst of its mystery. That is not always easy to do, but it is no more difficult than trying to comprehend the dimensions of a universe that are beyond my grasp.

Today I give thanks for a God that is so much bigger than we thought.

Chapter 5

All God's Creatures

Almost any conversation with me will eventually turn to animals. I cannot remember a time when I did not want a horse, and the moment that dream became a reality on my thirteenth birthday is as indelible as any memory can be.

I remember reviewing old family pictures with my mother years ago, and she expressed exasperation that most of them were of animals: this horse or that one, the dogs, the cows that my brother and I raised. When I was fourteen, we went to the bank and borrowed money to buy six cows, thus venturing into the ranching business with no experience whatsoever. My father was a pastor and he encouraged our entrepreneurship, but he didn't know the first thing about the cattle business.

These days I go to Siete Ranch, which is more of a retreat than a ranch, and pretend I am the rancher I would have wanted to be had I not been called into ministry. There is something extraordinarily peaceful and pastoral about being in a pasture with cows when the sun is about to set. But, more than anything else, there are the horses. That connection is spiritual, and I can't explain it anymore than anyone else can. Except to say, "Nowhere in the world am I happier than astride a horse."

7 The Dance

It is very early, and the morning is still relatively cool. Driving to Siete Ranch, I've opened the windows in my pickup and turned off the air-conditioner. I am enjoying my preferred method for staying cool—what my father-in-law called "God's air-conditioning." Leaves of hay, left over from the bales I hauled last week, are sucked out of the bed of the truck and into the cab through the rear sliding window, infusing the air with the unmistakable basil-like aroma of alfalfa. I inhale deeply and am instantly transported back to a time and place that I will never forget.

It was my thirteenth birthday, over fifty years ago. I was leading my brand-new horse into a stall at the barn of Chester Fields and found myself suddenly enveloped in the sights and sounds and smells of what I had always wanted to be. The smell of hay married to the unique smells of horses and barns and sweat and manure produced an extraordinary and uniquely appealing aroma. I had finally arrived.

Within the hour I will be sitting atop my new mare Bella, and the world will be so transformed that I will see it once again through the eyes of a child. Together we will listen for the music and strive for the perfect dance, that elusive waltz where human and beast are in perfect harmony. We probably won't achieve it but for a step or two, but we will come close enough to know that it is possible, and in those moments the world around us will become transfixed in a kind of near-perfection. The ancient voices will be heard, from Alexander the Great astride his stallion Bucephalus to the Comanche and the Kiowa on their war ponies—all whispering through the ages about the dance, about perfection.

In the dog days of summer, as I approach the final season of my own life, the truth emerges that the thirteen-year-old boy still lives deep within me. Nowhere in the world am I happier than astride a horse. So it has been since the days before memory, and so it will always be.

7 Puppy

There is a wild dog that has been hanging out at Siete Ranch for a couple of months. The first time I saw her at a great distance, I thought she was a coyote. She moved and acted like a coyote, and she displayed the extreme caution one sees only in a predator that sometimes becomes the prey.

I named the dog Puppy and decided I would make friends with her. Through the years my wife, Bobby, and I have fed numerous squirrels and rabbits out of our hands, and I thought that taming a dog would be easy. I started leaving food for her, but after a month I still could not get within a hundred yards of her. She was the most cautious domestic animal I have ever seen, and more cautious than most wild animals. But I give her credit: She is a survivor.

Last week I began riding my horse around her, and she allowed me to get within twenty-five yards or so. Any closer and she was gone. I had begun to give up hope that she might one day trust me. Last night she came to the barn to get her food while I was out there, keeping one eye on me (at a distance of about fifteen yards) while she ate her dog food. I carefully threw her part of a hot dog. She darted away, but quickly returned, trying out the wiener and deciding that this was her kind of meal. Long story short, within ten minutes she had her paws on my legs and was eating out of my hands.

I don't know what Puppy's history is, but I suspect that it is not so different from that of many people. At some point she became so wounded that she believed she would have to go it alone in order to survive. She decided that the act of trusting another living being would be far too dangerous to attempt. Her options in life had become extremely narrow, reduced to finding enough food and water to exist, and nothing more.

Now she has discovered the abundant life, complete with a banquet table set just for her and a companion who will look after her. I now have trouble working on my tractor because she is constantly there, trying to lick me in the face. She has discovered that she was born for relationships, and her joy can be seen in the wagging tail when I arrive on the scene.

I am beginning to understand why the act of trusting God can seem so simple but be so difficult for us humans. I wonder if, in similar fashion, God is waiting for you and me to discover the fullness of our relationship with the One who gives us life and gives it abundantly.

7- A Promise Kept

When I was a kid all I wanted was a horse. I can never remember not wanting one, so I guess it all started about age three or four. On every Christmas, every birthday, and every falling star, I wished only for one thing. I used to dream about waking up and finding a pony in the backyard.

My parents would have gotten me a horse if they could have. We lived in Dallas, and they understood, as I did not, that buying the horse was the easy part. The hard part came later when you had to feed it and have a place for it to stay. Life in the city was not conducive to a rural lifestyle. Nevertheless, I persisted. Oftentimes we would be driving in the country and would pass a pasture full of horses, and I could hardly contain my frustration: "There's a whole pasture of horses and nobody is even riding them! Why doesn't some nice person just *give* a horse to a kid who would take care of it?" I promised myself that if I ever got a chance to help a kid have a horse, I would do so.

It has been many years since I got my first horse, but I finally had a chance to make good on that long-ago promise. I found myself with a really nice horse in my pasture that I no longer rode, and so I advertised in the *Livestock Weekly*: "Free Horse to a Good Home." I conducted telephone interviews with more than fifty people and, frankly, I wish I had a horse to give to nearly all of them. Most were grandparents who wanted a safe horse for their grandkids, but there were several old cowboys in their eighties who were looking for "one more good horse" before they died.

The winner, however, was a place in Huntsville, Texas, called Camp Coyote, a nonprofit camp for kids. Its mission is to "provide a safe, fun-filled summer encouraging Christian morals and values," undergirded by the philosophy that "it is better to build boys and girls than to mend men and women." When the people at Camp Coyote heard about some of the outreach ministries of my church, they immediately sweetened the deal by offering two scholarships to participants in our mentoring program called Project Hope.

The following Monday afternoon at 5:30 Peppy stepped out of my trailer and into Camp Coyote's trailer for the ride to his new home. He had been a great traveling companion for me, and so there was a moment of sadness. However, it was nothing compared to the joy of making good on a promise that I made so many years ago, knowing that kids who can't own a horse will get to ride one. As a bonus, it allowed Project Hope participants to have the experience of a lifetime. For me, this was as good as it gets.

7 Spur Tracks

A while ago I decided to put my old saddle on my new mare. It had been quite a while since I had ridden this saddle, and I couldn't help noticing the spur tracks across the seat as I saddled up Bella. For the uninitiated, spur tracks are the marks that the rowels on your spurs make on your saddle during an unscheduled dismount. I've had a number of those through the years, and I could not remember which horse or which wreck left these particular tracks. But the reminder is there forever. There's an old cowboy belief that you never get bucked off or thrown from your horse; you should always ride the horse regardless of what happens. If you don't, then you just fell off your horse. But the truth of the matter is that, sooner or later, we all get thrown.

Life does that to us as well. And those incidents have a way of leaving their own spur tracks. They might not be as visible as the ones on my saddle, but most of us carry with us the inner scars of those moments when we somehow wound up in a wreck: maybe it was a lost job or lost relationship, it might have been the death of a loved one, or perhaps it was a deep struggle with addiction or mental illness. The wreck might have been in the past, but the scars remain.

Here's the good news: I had forgotten how good that old saddle rides. It has a great seat, and the stirrups hang just right. That saddle and I both have the scars that come with age, but with age that saddle has gained some character as well. I hope the same can be said of me.

7 RH2

Sitting on the front porch at Siete Ranch watching the cows as they grazed, I started thinking about RH2. Several years ago a friend and I decided to get back into the cow business. Both of us had raised cows as kids, but now we needed something for our midlife crises.

Jim found a set of twelve nice heifers that we bought. They were pretty evenly matched except for the one with ear tag RH2. She was the runt of the litter, as we used to say. She was small and not as nice as the others. Since Jim found the cows I insisted that he pick first. We both knew that I would end up with RH2. I didn't mind because the others were so nice.

That was a number of years ago. Jim has gone on to develop quite a sophisticated Hereford cattle operation, but not one of those six cows is in his herd. I have only a few cows, but the only one I have of those original six is RH2. The others have all been culled. As luck would have it, RH2 was the best cow of the lot.

She breeds right away, carries a calf with no problem, calves with ease and on time, and is the best mama cow I've ever seen. I don't have to worry about coyotes with RH2. On top of everything else, she grew into a decent size and puts outstanding calves on the ground. Turns out that RH2 was the pick of the litter.

If you've done much reading in the Bible, you know that God has a way of surprising us in that way. One of the best stories in the Old Testament is about God sending Samuel to Jesse to pick a new king for Israel (see 1 Samuel 16:1-13). He looked at Jesse's fine, strong sons and thought any of them could be a king, but God rejected them all. Then Samuel asked Jesse if there were any others, and Jesse conceded that David was out in the pasture tending sheep. He was the youngest, the smallest, the runt of the litter, but David was God's choice.

That story is repeated in the Bible many times, including God going to an uneducated teenager named Mary in an unremarkable little place called Nazareth (see Luke 1:26-27). For whatever reason, God sometimes chooses the last and least to play the most important roles in his plans for the future.

RH2 is a great reminder of the truth found so powerfully throughout the Bible: Don't judge people by appearance, breeding, education, or social standing. You never know who God might pick to make an enormous difference in your life or perhaps in the building of the Kingdom.

7- Save Us a Place

There is a veterinarian in our church who practices a rather touching protocol when he is called upon to euthanize a dog. A friend wrote to tell me that this vet has put two of her beloved dogs down in the past five years. Both times, just before giving them the shot, he kissed them and said, "Save us a place."

My theological position on this is pretty well known. The Bible tells us that God created everything there is, including our animals and pets. It also tells us that God is love, and much of the New Testament is about love.

As anyone who has ever had a dog for a pet can testify, that relationship really is about love. In fact, most dogs have much to teach us about the ineffable concept of unconditional love. Even when your spouse is mad at you, your dog still loves you. Unconditionally. Therefore, dogs go to heaven. Period.

You may be thinking that heaven is going to get real crowded for those of us who are animal lovers. I confess that there are all sorts of practical issues about heaven I haven't got figured out yet, including multiple marriages, whether or not there really are golf courses, and what to do about crazy Aunt Edna if she's up there. But I figure these are all minor issues for God, and that I should be focused on the primary task of just making the trip in the first place. On that score it is comforting to know that I've sent a few good dogs and horses on ahead who are, hopefully, saving me a place.

7- Horses

I spend some of my spare time riding horses. It is a passion. I don't raise horses or breed them. I don't show them in the ring. I just ride them and try to train them a bit.

I have discovered that horses have taught me more than I have taught them. For instance, they have taught me to be observant. Since the only language a horse has is body language, you have to be really observant in order to understand what it is he is telling you. The best horse trainers can almost read a horse's mind by watching his body language. My horses have taught me to be observant of them, but they have also taught me to be more sensitive to what I see in nature, in other people, and in the environment around me.

Horses, contrary to popular opinion, are very smart. It's just that they live in the moment rather than calculating the future. A good trainer can therefore teach a horse to do just about anything, but the technique must be very focused. If a horse does something right he will know it and learn from it if you reward him immediately. And by that I mean instantaneously. If you wait thirty seconds to reward him, he won't make the connection between what he did right and the reward. The same is true for discipline. Any discipline that doesn't come instantaneously just feels like punishment to the horse.

That leads me to my final and most important observation: In training a horse, it is much more effective to catch a horse doing something right and reward him than to catch him doing something wrong and discipline him. Discipline is occasionally necessary, but it is inferior to affirmation. Occasionally, I have the opportunity to ride with my friend Jack Brainard, one of the best western-horse trainers in America, and I am always amazed at his capacity to catch me doing something right when I know I am doing most things wrong. The results in terms of motivation are enormous.

I am aware that there is a difference between horses and people. Nevertheless, this is a lesson that works both in the equine and human worlds. I'm going to work more on catching people doing things right—from the kid at the drive-in burger place to my grandson to the people I work with—than doing things wrong. It's a really simple way of making life better and more joyful, don't you think?

7 Deer Tracks in the Arena

I have a riding arena at Siete Ranch that is fenced on all four sides. One day not long ago, I noticed something quite odd as I was leading a horse out of the barn: there were animal tracks in the freshly groomed sand of the arena. I checked both gates and discovered they were latched tight. How could there be animal tracks in a fenced space, but no animals?

Upon closer inspection, I solved the mystery. A deer or two had evidently jumped the fence, run a couple of laps around the arena, and then jumped out. I have seen deer only rarely at Siete Ranch, and so I kinda got a kick out of the fact that they had been playing in my arena. I am pleased that there are a few deer who call Siete Ranch home.

As I look back over the years I see lots of tracks left by those who call our church home and who have worked to make it a place that changes lives. There are thousands of volunteers, and I don't get to witness all that they do, but they leave tracks everywhere. For instance, I came up one Sunday and all the Advent decorations were up, the simple gift of volunteers who moved in and silently did their jobs without fanfare or thanks. I went to the Project Hope Christmas party and heard testimonies about lives changed because of coaches and mentors who, unnamed and unrecognized, helped individuals transform the way they live and work. I could go on, and so could you. All around us are the tracks of those who selflessly make our homes and churches and communities more decent places to live.

Will Durant, challenged to sum up civilization in half an hour, did it in less than a minute:

"Civilization is a stream with banks. The stream is sometimes filled with blood from people killing, stealing, shouting and doing the things historians usually record, while on the banks, unnoticed, people build homes, make love, raise children, sing songs, write poetry, and even whittle statues. The story of civilization is the story of what happened on the banks." (Jim Hicks, "More History from the Will Durants: Spry Old Team Does It Again," *Life* [October 18, 1963]: 92)

Let me say thanks to all those who silently and selflessly walk through our lives and leave things just a little bit better than before.

7 Mama Cows

Early one week I loaded two steers into my trailer and drove them off of Siete Ranch to be weaned. I had to leave the mother cows, RH2 and M6, locked in the working pens to keep them from following me down the road, out the gate, and out on to the highway. RH2 especially has a very maternal nature, and she would have followed the truck and trailer for as many miles as her legs would take her.

I have done this on many occasions, and I never fail to be struck by the powerful maternal instinct that is found in so many creatures. And I can't help but speculate on what it says to us about the creation. There is a growing atheist movement in this country that would like to convince us we are no more than the composite of certain molecular processes that have grown more complex through the ages. We are told that life blossomed not because of a Creator, but out of sheer chance, and that it has evolved because of the instinct for survival. But all you have to do is separate a mama cow from her baby, and you know that there is more to it than that.

As far as I'm concerned, the Bible gives us an explanation that comes much closer to the reality we observe. The Bible tells us that there was a Creator who breathed life into the world. Whether that took seven days or many centuries is beside the point. It helps to elucidate something that we all know: we have feelings such as compassion and love that cannot be traced to molecular structure. We have the capacity for sacrifice and heroism that cannot be explained by natural selection. We have yearnings and ideals, we dream dreams and hear songs and write poetry, not because of some biological imperative but because there is something about our nature that can only be described as spiritual, something that was bestowed upon us by the Creator.

There is no doubt that we live in a fallen world. All you have to do is turn on the news to learn of the many ways in which we turn the created order back into chaos. But RH2 reminds us that our true nature is to protect the young, to care for one another, to manifest in our words and actions the love of the One who created us.

7- Horse Language

Little known fact (maybe): horses understand Spanish better than English. Well, maybe it's not a fact, but it is a long-held theory of mine. I've always talked to my horses in Spanish, using what limited vocabulary I have. It doesn't take much—just a few words to tell them what good horses they are or that they are doing a maneuver correctly. I promise you, they understand Spanish better and find it to be more soothing and reassuring than English. At least that's my theory.

I once owned a gelding named Caballo del Rio, which means horse of the river. I called him Caballo for short. One day I was riding alongside the San Gabriel River in Georgetown, Texas, when a small group of Spanish-speaking children started running behind me calling in excited voices, "Caballo! Caballo!" At first I was quite perplexed at how they could possibly know my horse's name, and then I realized that they were merely shouting "horse, horse," as would almost any group of young children. That reaction is pretty universal in any language. But *Caballo* sounds much more natural; even anonymous children knew him by name.

Little-known fact (for real): Jesus usually spoke in an ancient language called Aramaic. That was his natural tongue, not Hebrew or Greek. Nevertheless, there is something universal about his message regardless of the language or dialect. When he says, "Allow the children to come to me..." (Matthew 19:14 CEB) or "Neither do I condemn you. Go, and from now on, don't sin anymore" (John 8:11 CEB) we all seem to recognize that he is speaking to us and that he has found words that are soothing and reassuring in any language. We sense that the message is profoundly personal in spite of the fact that it has been received and embraced in thousands of languages and dialects.

The truth is, I don't really know that horses understand Spanish better than English. What I do know is that with both horses and people, in Spanish or English or any other language, words of reassurance and love are the most important words we ever speak.

Chapter 6

Priorities

My drives between my place of work and Siete Ranch give me plenty of "soak" time to think about what is truly important and what is not. One would think that after all the hours I've spent in my pickup truck, I would have things figured out by now. Unfortunately, I am compelled to report a mission not yet completed on that score. But I can tell you that God invested awesome power in every one of us by granting us the freedom to choose. That freedom is both the burden and the glory of being human.

How do we balance the necessity of earning money and enjoying material goods with spending enough time with our families and helping those who are in need? How do we embrace all the exciting things life has to offer, while still taking time to enjoy the simplest pleasures in life? How do we choose to think about all of the conflicting values and attractions that life presents to us? What did Jesus mean when he said, "Seek ye first the kingdom of God, and his righteousness; and all these things shall be added unto you" (Matthew 6:33 KJV)?

I am clear about the fact that I will never have all these answers, but my reflections on these things have yielded some guiding principles. I know that neither material success nor things will ultimately bring one happiness, but that they are not evil in and of themselves. I know that sometimes just sitting is the best thing you can do for yourself. And I know that one of the high callings in life is to wrestle with all these questions about what is truly important and what is not.

7- Things

I remember when my three-and-a-half-year-old grandson Liam got a new pair of tennis shoes. They were Spider-Man shoes and had those little red lights on them that blinked when he walked. He was so excited about them that he insisted on wearing them to bed. The next morning he practically danced down the stairs, still wearing his pajamas and tennis shoes.

I couldn't help admiring the way he experienced such sheer joy over this minor wardrobe change, and it occurred to me that perhaps it says something important to us about our relationships with the material things in our lives. After all, Jesus said that we must become like children if we are to enter the kingdom of God; that has always been an attractive theological statement for me.

The typical religious comment on our relationship with things is usually pretty negative. We have allowed material things to overtake our lives, our budgets, and our common sense. Our stuff now owns us rather than the other way around. Our material greed has placed us in too much debt, and our grasping for material objects compromises our search for spiritual meaning. We should be hungry for spiritual blessings rather than material blessings.

As far as I know, all of those things are true. I believe them, and I have preached them for many years. But I don't think they tell the full story. My observation of young children hints at a further truth that we ignore at our peril. There is nothing inherently evil in the material possessions of our lives, nor in our enjoyment of them. They only take on demonic characteristics when we allow our pursuit of them, sometimes even our lust for them, to control us and cause us to lose sight of the important realities in life. The greatest evidence of that can often be seen in the fact that what we long for gives us little pleasure once it is acquired.

To be personal about this, my problem is not that I have things, but that they don't necessarily bring me the joy I was anticipating. Perhaps I have too many things. Or maybe too many expectations about what they might accomplish for me. I'm trying to learn from my grandson the simple gift of enjoying what I have without being burdened by the absence of what I don't have. If you see me wearing lighted tennis shoes and dancing, you will know I am making progress.

7 Sitting

I read some advice the other day that prompted me to think about the fact that we don't sit anymore. I don't mean that we don't spend hours at a time in a chair or on a recliner, working a computer or watching television. I mean we don't just sit, taking in the wonders of God's universe or contemplating the goodness of life. Some people might call that meditation or prayer, but I like the idea of just calling it sitting, without any agenda other than allowing God to speak to us in whatever way God might choose.

Here's the advice I read: practice sitting for at least ten minutes every day. In other words, take ten minutes every day and turn off the television or radio, shut down the computer, and put down the book. Go to the park or the creek, the patio or porch, or even the quietest room in your house, and just sit. You might close your eyes or keep them open, you might meditate or hum a tune, you might pray or empty your mind of all the clutter. Sit for ten minutes without worrying or problem-solving, and see what happens.

I practiced this the other day on the front porch at Siete Ranch. It's something I used to do all the time but had gotten out of the habit. I have, by design, no television at Siete, but a computer has become a necessity. The pressures of a very busy year have found me sitting more and more in front of the computer and less and less on the front porch. Siete Ranch had become my office away from the office rather than my retreat.

On this day I left the computer even though the work was unfinished, and I practiced sitting on the front porch. Here is what I learned: Sitting is God's work. Maybe the best way to put it is to say it is God's time to work on us, but it doesn't happen until we take the time to be still. David put it this way: "Be still, and know that I am God!" (Psalm 46:10 NRSV).

I don't know about you, but I have to be reminded that the busier I am, the more important it is to practice the simple things of life. Sitting is at the top of that list.

７ Stop!

Have you ever noticed that *stop* is one of the first words young children learn to read? It is because it is written on those big red signs at thousands of street corners around the country. Kids love those signs because they are easy to read and their meaning is easy for children to understand.

I have come to believe that most of us need spiritual stop signs that will force us to disengage for a while. You can interpret that sentence in the way that most fits the challenges of your life. Perhaps you need to disengage from the ongoing argument with a spouse, the anxiety-producing competition with a coworker, or the relentless quest for more of something that you already have in abundance. A spiritual stop sign can be helpful in many ways.

Today, however, I hope you will think about the power of that word as it relates to the frantic and nonstop activity we engage in. Most of us rush all day long from one meeting or activity to the next until we fall into bed exhausted. We try closing our eyes for a moment of prayer or meditation, and the next thing we know the alarm clock is going off.

And so here is my challenge: When you finish reading this chapter put some stop signs in your day. Go ahead and type them into your Outlook calendar (or whatever you use to keep yourself organized). Find five or ten minutes between meetings, or make it the first and/or last appointment of the day. Just use the word *stop* and, when you come to that moment in your day, turn off your phone, close your door, pull down whatever application is up on your computer, and do nothing. That's right; do nothing. Let the silence take over that moment, and trust that God will be there in the silence.

Giving up the need to be constantly busy might be the first step toward spiritual well-being.

7 Thoughts from Siete Ranch

DO celebrate the gift of life every day, including the small things like flowers and trees and cool breezes.

DON'T worry about the failures of the past. God has already both forgiven and forgotten them.

DO care passionately about the world and the people around you, and know that your God-given gifts can make a big difference.

DON'T sweat the small stuff.

DO remember that it is more about the journey than the destination.

DON'T travel alone.

7 Slow Down

Entering the city limits of the little town of Tioga, Texas from the north, I noticed him too late. Sitting deep in the right-of-way on the west side of the road, partly hidden by trees, the city police officer had already clocked my speed. Looking at my speedometer, I observed I was exceeding the speed limit by about eight miles per hour. Then something happened I think I will always remember and appreciate. He hit his flashing red lights as a warning and waved me on.

Admitting my self-interest, it nevertheless occurred to me that this was an example of law enforcement at its best. But I also thought that it serves as an interesting metaphor for some of the real challenges we face in life. There may be some cities where most of the people need to pick up the pace, so to speak, but where I live is not one of them. Most of us in my town (and I suspect most of my readers elsewhere) need to seriously consider the advantages of slowing down just a bit. A friendly warning here and there might be more than appropriate.

I have more than a few friends who have received that warning from their personal physician or cardiologist. Occasionally someone will get the message from their spouse or therapist. It is best not to receive the message from an emergency room doctor.

One of the best reasons I know of for attending church regularly is that it forces one to slow down for at least one hour. Even if the sermon is mediocre or the choir is less than spectacular, a worship service is a great place to stop and ponder what is truly important in one's life. It can serve as a kind of spiritual traffic cop that warns us to slow down before there are serious consequences. It is a time for one to think deeply about life, about priorities, and about things eternal.

I think there are a lot of people who think of God as a relentless traffic cop who is sitting around waiting to catch us doing something wrong. My Tioga policeman offers another vision: someone who just wants us to stay safe out there.

7 The Other Side of the Fence

Driving down FM 1385, I came across a sight not that un-familiar to those who spend much time in the country. A large Black Angus cow had her head stuck between the third and fourth strands of a barbed-wire fence and was practically de-stroying it in order to graze the grass on the right-of-way. She acted like she was eating dessert at a four-star restaurant, even though she was standing in lush native grass on her side of the fence. If you have spent time around cows or horses, you know there is no mystery about where the expression "The grass is always greener on the other side of the fence" comes from.

Given the supposition that humans have a much more high-ly developed cerebral cortex than do bovines, one would think we would be immune to this kind of faulty thinking. But, as we all know, the other-side-of-the-fence mentality runs rampant in species Homo sapiens. I have rarely—*very* rarely—observed a human being who appeared to be unfazed by the attractions that appear to be inherent in another job, another home, another re-lationship, another church, or social group. My father-in-law, after returning from over three years of combat in WWII, was content with all that he had until he died at age eighty-seven. He was not a perfect human being, but his character was unas-sailable on this point, and by that virtue I'm quite sure he has a special place in the Kingdom.

As for myself, I am especially vulnerable to the apparent seductions of other towns, especially small rural towns. I can hardly drive through one, much less eat the lunch special at the local café, without succumbing to the belief that the local residents have somehow found paradise and are smart enough to keep the secret to themselves. If it happens that more patrons are wearing spurs than not, I'm always tempted to drive by the local United Methodist church and speculate as to whether it appears prosperous enough to support my admittedly exorbitant lifestyle. I will leave it to you to ruminate about your own short-comings on this subject.

The Old Testament tells us not to covet. Jesus encouraged us to be content with what we have. The old hymn says to count our blessings "one by one." Our faith speaks powerfully about this particular temptation. As for me, observing the greedy fool-ishness of that cow is pretty powerful medicine. Who, after all, wants to look that stupid?

7 The Cutting Edge

As you know, I like to think of myself as being on the cut-ting edge of technology. Of course that is my standing joke, but it is true that I got my first cell phone in 1986. By most standards, that makes me a very early user. And that's not all. I don't have an iPad, but I have a computer. I don't have an iPhone, but I have a BlackBerry. So, I may not be cool, but I don't consider myself to be an anachronism when it comes to functional technology.

But here is the rub—and I have discovered that it is a seri-ous impediment to being considered cool. I *use* my phone. By that I mean I still like to dial phone numbers and speak words into the phone. I have come to recognize that this is extremely old fashioned. I exasperate many of my friends and colleagues because I still call them and communicate verbally rather than by texting. These are what I call conversations and it seems very intuitive to me. But I am relinquishing any claim that I might have to being "cool."

What's odd about this is that I'm not a very social person. My first experiment with Facebook alerted me to how truly socially phobic I am. The moment I started being deluged with messages from other people, I closed my account. Likewise, I don't like talking just to be talking, but the phone has always been a very efficient way for me to get things done. These days, I feel silly talking on a telephone, but I'm not sure that I (or my thumbs) can adapt to exchanging a lot of information by way of texting.

When I first started writing this, I think my primary motivation was to gain sympathy. I'm just sure that lots of you agree with me. But the more I consider it, I believe I want to start a counter-revolution. Just think about this: if the phone technology had begun with texting, and then progressed to actual voice conversations, wouldn't we think of texting as being regressive and primitive? I'm sure of it. So I say let's stand up for progress! Let's move into the golden age of technology! Let's start using our phones for what they were created to be! Won't you join me on the cutting edge of technology? Just give somebody a call right now and try having a real conversation.

7- Showers

Because of some responsibilities I have that are beyond the local church, I spent yesterday on the phone. When I say

I spent the day on the phone, I mean I spent the *whole* day on the phone. Other than a one-hour staff meeting, I was talking, texting, or e-mailing with people around the country. For lunch I ate a sandwich while standing up and talking on the phone.

Because the communication had been so intense, I had not had an opportunity to look at the news, the stock market, or the weather. Nor had I bothered to open the blinds and look out the windows of my office. About 4:30 PM I was returning to my office from our finance office, where I had dropped off a receipt. I had accomplished this little chore while wearing a headphone and talking on my BlackBerry. Because I was going through the atrium, I glanced out the windows at the fountain and courtyard on the east side of our building and was shocked to see that it was raining. Pouring. The bright, hot sun I had seen early that morning had been replaced by dark clouds and buckets of rain, which we desperately needed.

When I returned to my office I took off my earbuds, muted my BlackBerry, turned off the lights, and sat down to have a conversation with God. It went something like this: "God, I confess that I have been busy, busy, busy today. I have been seduced (once again!) into believing that my work is more important than your work. My view of your world has been so limited and confined today that I have failed to notice that you are blessing us with much-needed rain. And I want you to know that I get the message: you are showering us with blessings all the time, perhaps most intensely at those times when we are so distracted that we fail to see you at work in our world and in our lives. Help me to always keep my eyes and ears open so that I might be able to hear the raindrops of your presence, see the showers of your blessings, feel the abundance of your grace."

I confess that God usually does not audibly answer my prayers. This time was an exception. As I closed my prayer and opened my eyes, I could hear the muffled sounds of raindrops hitting the roof above me. Showers of blessings. Amazing grace. The ancient Word being proclaimed.

7 — Fasting

If you made some commitments to yourself about spiritual practice during the season of Lent and are having trouble keeping them, I'm about to make you feel a whole lot better.

I decided to try fasting, something I've never done before, along with practicing a little meditation, which I have done before with very meager results. The problem with meditation is that it requires you to turn your mind off. I can't do that when I go to sleep, so it has always been a challenge for me.

I've heard and read through the years that fasting facilitates meditation. The old saints would talk about reaching a point in their fast where they felt detached from the world, in a kind of spiritual zone. I have friends and colleagues who speak about the same thing. So I thought I'd give it a try. I've been fasting from noon on Wednesday till noon on Thursday.

Here is what I meditated about this morning: eggs, bacon, and hash browns, with some pancakes on the side. Following the timeless instructions of yoga instructors and others, I quickly brushed those thoughts from my mind and focused on my breathing. Breathe in, breathe out. Within a few seconds I was meditating on my plans for grilling steaks tonight (as a reward for my fasting)...breathe in, breathe out...slicing into a rib eye, noticing that it is a perfect medium rare...breathe in, breathe out...putting extra sour cream on the baked potato (as a reward for my fasting)...breathe in, breathe out...I think you get the idea.

I'm not yet ready to call it quits, but I am questioning the wisdom of combining fasting with meditation. Or maybe I need to admit the obvious: I am no saint. Not even close.

Come to think of it, isn't that the point of Lent? Acknowledging that we are not yet who God would have us be, and offering thanks for the grace of God who fills in our weak places and makes us whole in spite of our brokenness.

In the final analysis our salvation does not rest with our ability to breathe in, breathe out, but with our knowledge that it is God who breathed into us the gift of life in the first place; it is God who saves us by grace alone; it is God who, in spite of all our weaknesses and wanderings, loves us fully and brings us home.

Chapter 7

The Circle of Life

Members of my church have heard me say many times that "if I am lucky enough to get to the Pearly Gates, I darn sure have some questions I'd like answered." As a minister one of the hardest things I have had to deal with is all the *why* questions. Why did my loved one die? Why my child? Why the young wife or husband with so much to live for? Why the beloved friend or parent who should have had many more years to share?

Many years ago, I was visiting people in a nursing home in Burkburnett, Texas, right after the tragic death of a young man who was known and loved by nearly everyone in town. A woman who was approaching ninety years of age asked me the most difficult question I've ever been asked: "Pastor Don, why won't God take me? I've been praying for years for God to take me home. Why did God choose John rather than me?" I sat there, holding her hand, the two of us lost in the profoundest of mysteries.

While I don't have the answers to these questions, I do know that death is a part of life, and that we can grow spiritually and in our relationships with others by paying attention to what it has to teach us. I am profoundly grateful to my mother and so many others who have taught me about both living and dying. Even my young grandson Liam is starting his journey with this, the greatest of mysteries.

7 The Lizard

The lizard was dead. My three-year-old grandson Liam took me by the hand and led me out to the patio to visit the body. He had discovered it earlier in the afternoon. He was neither afraid nor sad but, as is common with children his age, fascinated. This was a new experience for him, this thing we refer to as death. He wanted to touch the lizard, but he didn't want to touch it. He wanted to pick it up, but he was afraid to.

He wanted to know what we should do with it. I suggested that we should throw it into the bushes next to the house: dust to dust, ashes to ashes, I explained. But his better human instincts—even at age three—kicked in. Somehow this didn't seem appropriate to him. And so the lizard remained lying in state until later in the day when Liam's attention had spun off into a new direction. I then sent the lizard into the hollies, blessing it with a little prayer for the journey.

And thus began my grandson's lifelong dance with the issue of mortality, this mystery of life and death. It is hard for me to bear the thought, but I know that in the not-too-distant future he will confront this mystery again in the form of a beloved pet, and there will be the added dimension of personal sadness and loneliness. Then, inevitably, will come the loss of a grandparent or a special teacher. Tragedy might even befall one of his classmates. I know the longer he dances with death the more difficult it will become and death will not be a partner he chooses but rather the one he is stuck with. Sooner or later the dance will force him to ponder his own mortality and that of those whom he loves the most.

It *is* the great and profound mystery of our lives, isn't it? But, painful as it is, our dance with death, our own experience of mortality, can make us better humans. It can force us to pay more attention to that which is of real importance in life. Death may be the partner we do not choose, but ultimately it is the partner that teaches us how to dance and how to live, reminding us that every step should be a celebration of God's holy gifts.

7· Her Final Gift

When my mother was told that she had only a matter of weeks to live, she responded with the same calm strength and equanimity she had demonstrated all of her life. She kindly thanked the doctor for his care and his candor. She went to the funeral home and picked out her own casket so that "the boys won't spend too much," and then she got back to the business of living. She went shopping, cooked for her family, entertained friends, and attended church until she was too weak. We had a grand time of living during those three months.

All cancer should be called brain cancer because it takes over the brains of everyone touched by it. It invades your thoughts, your dreams, and every waking moment not filled with doing the necessities of living. It changes your life. But my mother decided that if it was to change our lives, it would do so in a positive way by helping us reorder our priorities and see what is truly important.

And for us, her family, she set a great example. She stared

the great enemy straight in the eye and never blinked. Her calm and strong faith reassured us that, though death can take much from you, it cannot take from you that which is most important. In that discovery you begin to taste the exhilaration of life lived on the edge, the sweetness of life lived for the moment, and the joy of a life that comes from God as pure gift.

My mother always taught us how to live. During her last days she taught us how to die, how to face death with dignity and courage and strength. As I now ponder all that has happened, I realize that her final gift to us was to teach us how to get back to the joy of living even after experiencing what seems to be unbearable sorrow. And I know that, somewhere on the other side, she joins me in saying, "Thanks be to God."

7- Small Things

A friend responded to one of my columns based on my memory of the taste of well water. It had brought back powerful recollections for him, and he commented that, as he read, he could "smell" the well water of his youth and could see, in his mind's eye, all the kids lined up for the washing routine.

His next statement was, I thought, rather powerful. He said that when we come to the end of life and look back, it will not necessarily be the big things that made the difference, but rather the small things. We live life for the most part believing that it is the big victories or big defeats, the big salaries (or lack of), the major recognitions and trophies (or lack of) that really count. We worry about big things like the stock market, the job market, or the cattle market. But when we get closer to the end, we think back and cherish the small things that made the difference between a life wasted and a life well-lived.

Those are wise words.

I might as well go ahead and tell you about those back-porch dinners at the farm. My grandmother, aunt, and mother would set the table on the screened-in back porch. There would be a red-checkered tablecloth, and the table would be filled with fried chicken and country ham, both yellow corn and white corn, both corn bread and corn "light" bread, fresh peas they had shelled that morning, and iced tea. Both cake and pie were served for dessert. When the dinner bell was rung, nobody was late.

If you grew up on a farm or ranch, you know that dinner was what occurred at noon, and supper was what took place in the evening. This next sentence will surely bring back memories. After dinner was finished, the women would leave everything on the table and take a big table cloth and cover it to keep the flies off. There it stayed until we returned for the evening meal to eat the leftovers.

What seems to be a minor memory looms large in my soul. I think that if there were just one scene I could re-create out of my decades of living, it would not be my college graduation, the district football championship, or the day we moved into the new sanctuary. It would be just one more meal on the screened-in back porch, the taste of fresh-shelled peas and my grandmother's relish...the family gathered just one more time.

7 A Bad Day

I hate to admit this, but when my grandson was four he got expelled from preschool. Not exactly expelled, but close enough. Since my office was in the adjacent building, the administrators called and hinted that I might want to come and get him. The alternative, they suggested, was to bring in a SWAT team.

Since it is my assumption that my grandson Liam might one day want to apply for a job or even obtain a security clearance, I'm not going to tell you all the things he had done. In fact, I have negotiated the deal so that the record of that day is now sealed forever. Let's just say he pretty much terrorized the teachers first and then took on the entire administrative staff. Once I got him he was fine because I bought him ice cream. I don't have a teaching certificate, but I do understand the power of a bribe.

When I asked him what went wrong in class, he was very matter-of-fact about it: "I was having a bad day." I congratulated him on recognizing that fact, and then we talked about some optional behaviors he might choose when having a bad day. Relatively speaking, he was much more focused on the ice cream than the discussion about alternative behaviors.

Here's the good news, and the reason I am writing this. For the next few weeks, every day in school was a really good day. I can't guarantee all days will be good days forever, but I do know that for weeks the days were outstanding. And therein lies our hope: bad days don't last forever. You might have a string of bad days or even have months of bad days, but sooner or later the tide turns and bad days turn to good days. Having seen a few bad days myself, I honestly believe this to be a law of nature.

So, take it from Liam: if you are having a bad day, go buy yourself some ice cream. Ponder what you might do differently. And then be patient. Sooner or later, the laws of nature will be on your side.

7- Advent Resurrection

The disciples had been sitting around Jerusalem for three days. The crucifixion had wiped out all their hopes and dreams. In their understanding, Jesus was dead and buried, sealed forever in a tomb. It's not that they were struggling to find some thin sliver of hope. They were totally hopeless, finished, wondering what to do with the world in which they had been left. Then suddenly, Jesus was alive. The whole world looked different.

I hadn't thought about this until recently. If you read the Bible carefully you will discover that, for some reason, God chooses to bury things before resurrecting them. There was no reason why Jesus couldn't have just come down off the cross instead of being buried. But God chose for Jesus to stay in the tomb three days, just as God chooses for the wheat seed or the tulip bulb to stay buried in the cold winter ground for a period before it germinates and grows.

Perhaps you have noticed in your own life that the sense of resurrection does not come easily. It usually follows a period of despair and hopelessness. New life springs out of the darkness of winter.

It may seem odd to talk about Easter and Advent together, but in fact they are inexorably linked. The open tomb is the reason we know that our wintertime waiting is not hopeless. The coming of the babe of Bethlehem is our reminder that God does, inevitably, come. In the end God will come to restore earth to the perfection that was intended in the original creation. It will be the perfection of the Garden.

And so the liturgical seasons are all linked together in one great salvation drama. And our prayer, in each season of life, remains the same: "Come, Lord Jesus."

7- The Other Side of the Hill

My little group of friends was drinking coffee at Alice's Café in Marfa, Texas, and the subject of the "missing ones" came up. One of the regulars was moving to San Antonio in order to be closer to doctors, and everyone was clearly disappointed. Somebody said, "Seems like everyone is either moving off or we take them to the hill on the edge of town." The last half of that statement was sobering as we silently recalled the two that were buried in the past year.

If you stop and think about it, life is itself a weird and sobering experience. We work and work trying to achieve some made-up goals: a good job, a lasting marriage, a comfortable retirement, perhaps fame or wealth. But ultimately we all wind up in the "hill on the edge of town." Trying to make sense out of all of that is daunting to say the least. Trying to make sense out of it without some kind of faith, it seems to me, is impossible.

A theologian once said that Christianity can be divided into three major eras. The original church was driven by the search for the answer to death and the quest for eternal life. Starting with the Middle Ages, the church wrestled with the question of sin and how to be free from its burden. But the modern era, he said, is driven by the quest for meaning. It seems to me that the three questions can't be separated.

What I am clear about in my own mind is that the meaning of life is inextricably linked with what takes place beyond the grave, with a God who gracefully leads us into a new life of profound depth and meaning that is impossible for us to grasp in this life. But I also believe that the journey and the destination are not unrelated. The goal of this life is to live within the kingdom on earth as much as possible by loving as much as possible. That means loving God, loving life, and loving others. If we can do that well then the "other side of the hill" is something neither to be dreaded nor longed for, but merely the next stage in our journey with God.

7 Plotting the Resurrection

In his book *Longing for Enough in a Culture of More,* my friend Paul Escamilla quotes a comment made by author E. B. White about his wife. It was the autumn before her death and he observed her in the garden busily burying bulbs in the black earth "under those dark skies in the dying October, calmly plotting the resurrection" (*E. B. White: A Biography* [W. W. Norton & Co., 1986], 127; quoted in *Longing for Enough in a Culture of More* [Abingdon Press, 2007], 127).

That is an image powerful enough to remember for a life-time: this remarkable woman, entering the final season of her own life, yet convinced that an eternal spring will surely arrive for both her tulips and herself.

The secular critique of the Christian belief in resurrection is that it is "pie in the sky," that it ignores reality, and that it glosses over the darkness and tragedy of life. In fact, the biblical accounts do just the opposite. That is why we observe Good Friday as the darkest day in history, why we drape the cross, and why we read out loud about the cowardice of the disciples, the betrayal by Judas, and the unbelief of nearly every follower who saw or heard about the empty tomb.

The Easter message is not about a God who saves us from pain and darkness, but about a God who is plotting victory in the midst of defeat, who is planting seeds in the darkness of winter, and who is preparing a Technicolor palette for the painting of the blackest canvas.

If life has been unequivocally good and joyous for you recently, I expect that you might skip the Easter message and continue your journey with trips to the country club, the golf course, the family gathering, or the lake house. But if you, like most of us, have entered the tomb this past year, tasted defeat or betrayal or despair, or worried about your child or parent or marriage, the Easter message is of the highest priority. The Easter message is not about pie in the sky but about ordinary people who choose to "[plot] the resurrection" because of an extraordinary God whose promise of eternal life is rooted in the darkest of realities.

7 The Barbershop

It is Fat Tuesday, and I went to get my haircut today. As I sat in the chair, I started thinking about this monthly ritual that I have been following for over sixty years. It has changed a bit over time: the blow dryers, the women barbers and stylists, and the cost. But much remains the same. There is still a shoeshine station at the barbershop where I go, and my barber, Henry, still uses shave soap and a straight razor to trim my sideburns and neck.

I remember playing football when I was in high school in Denison. Denison was football crazy. If we lost on Friday night, we generally did not go downtown for a haircut the next day. This was before long hair for men was acceptable, and I've always been grateful for the fact that we won enough to keep from looking like hippies. But, believe me, I think we would have accepted the hippie look before being subjected to the barbershop analysis of the game.

My grandson has not yet had his first barbershop haircut. So far he has been kept trimmed by his grandmother Babba, who does a pretty respectable job wielding the scissors. But I'm thinking about starting him on the road to this lifelong manly ritual and am wondering if it will be the same for him sixty years from now: a place to shine your boots, the smell of old-time tonics and colognes, someone sweeping up the floor, and a barber who knows the old, classic way of trimming with a straight razor. For some reason it gives me comfort to think that it might be so.

Every Ash Wednesday I participate in an ancient tradition

that dates back to at least the tenth century. For me, it captures both the tone and the mystery of this remarkable season of Lent. Worship styles have changed dramatically in the past few years, but it seems to me that some of our oldest traditions are the ones that should be preserved for those who come after us. I can't help wondering if, sixty years from now, my grandson will be taking his family to church for the imposition of ashes. For some reason it gives me comfort to think that it might be so.

7 I Forgot

Thursday, 3:00 PM, my assistant calls me and asks, "Did you get my e-mail?"

"What e-mail?"

"The one I sent you reminding you about the deadline for your column. I'm supposed to be sending it out right now." Silence.

Well, I had obviously not checked my BlackBerry for the last couple of hours, and I had forgotten the deadline for my column. Such things happen more frequently these days. I forget where I left things. I forget about deadlines. I worry about forgetting parts of my sermon. I would forget nearly everything if it were not for the fact that I log most things into a calendar that I check frequently.

I honestly don't think I have some terrible disease. I looked up the definition of *dementia* and this is what I found: "A usually progressive condition (as Alzheimer's disease) marked by deteriorated cognitive functioning often with emotional apathy" (http://www.merriam-webster.com/dictionary/dementia). The fact that I felt compelled to look it up is a bit frightening, but I don't think it describes me, at least not yet. I think it's more like the hard disk is full or perhaps just needs reformatting. Whatever the reason, I just plain forgot.

So here's what I'm grateful for: a faithful and diligent assistant who saw to it that my column will arrive only hours late rather than days late or not at all. But as I think about all of this, I am also grateful for the knowledge that there is One who never forgets. The more I get in touch with my own fallibility, the more grateful I am for the faith that tells me there is a God who knows me fully, who accepts my shortcomings, and who still loves me. A God who never forgets who I am, where I came from, and what I'm dealing with.

There *may* come a day when full-blown dementia becomes my lot in life. There *will* come a day when I will lose control of my grasp on this life, when my earthly faculties will slip out of my control, when in order to move on I must let go. I am grateful for the knowledge that, when that day comes, there will be One who has never forgotten me and will greet me as a friend. That is one thing worth remembering.

7 Easter Afterglow

It is Wednesday night of Holy Week, and I am writing this column early. My thoughts drift back to another Wednesday of Holy Week. The year was 1987, and the date was April 15. My father had just died, and I was wandering around Methodist

Hospital in Houston. I was heartbroken even though we had known for almost two weeks that this would be the ultimate outcome of his illness.

We were getting ready to plan the funeral, which would be on Good Friday. Never had the Easter message been of more importance to me than at that moment. It was my faith in the risen Christ that sustained me. Because we buried my father on Good Friday, I have always felt that I could identify with the despair of the disciples on that first Good Friday and with their remarkable joy and hope of that first Easter Sunday when they learned that he had risen.

In this afterglow of Easter the power of the message has varying degrees of impact upon us. For you, perhaps, Easter was but a joyous occasion when family and friends got together, attended church, and celebrated a great religious tradition. But I can assure you that, for others, the power of this celebration is a matter of life or death, of hope or despair. And so it will be for you one day in the future.

Every year when we stand at the open tomb on Easter, we find ourselves in a new situation, with a new perspective on life. I urge you, as a personal witness, to never discount the great good news of Easter. It is the most powerful Word of my life, and it is a Word that I will proclaim until my time arrives to join that great cloud of witnesses who have gone before me.

Chapter 8

Our Daily Life

I have spent forty years trying to make the connection between God, faith, and our daily life. I think most church members believe I have this all figured out, and I'm just patiently trying to explain it to everyone else. The truth, of course, is that I'm struggling with it just like you or the guy down the street or in the cubicle next to yours. It's not always easy to understand how our relationship with God is related to the traffic jam we are stuck in or the work deadline we are facing.

Faith, including our individual experiences with God and prayer, is a truly personal matter. There is a reason you and I have often been warned to stay out of conversations that involve politics or religion. Nevertheless, at our best, we are sometimes able to witness to the mysterious power of God in our lives, and we are aware that this power enables us to, at least on occasion, do the simple and right thing.

My hope is that you will read the following reflections in the belief that God really does walk with you, and bless you, in your daily life.

7 One Person Is Missing

In the hallway outside our offices are a number of banners made by one of the confirmation classes a year or two ago. One of them depicts a picture of the earth in the shape of a heart, and surrounding the heart are stick figures of people holding hands. The big bold lettering on the banner proclaims the theme: BRINGING THE WORLD TOGETHER WITH LOVE.

Last Friday I walked by the banner and noticed something on the floor underneath it. One of the stick figures, which had been cut out of construction paper and pasted onto the banner, had slipped off. It was lying, like a fallen soldier, beneath the message for which it had given its life. As I looked at the banner, I noticed that there is no longer an unbroken chain of stick figures holding hands around the world. One person is missing.

That serves as an apt analogy for God's mission in the world, doesn't it? The kingdom of God isn't complete as long as there is one person missing. We will never have peace on earth as long as there is one person missing. We will never experience true justice as long as there is one person missing. Our churches will never be complete as long as there is one person missing. God's world demands an unbroken chain of people, holding hands and bringing the world together with love.

There have been times, I know, when I have been the missing person. I have fallen from the chain and lain at the foot of the world with no mission and no commitment. At times I have picked myself up and rejoined the chain, and at other times someone else has picked me up and held me up until I could do my part.

I'm glad I spotted the missing person, and I'm going to be more vigilant from now on. I invite you to join me. Pick yourself up, or perhaps pick someone else up when the opportunity presents itself. That, after all, is what the mission of God is all about.

7 Just Do It

My suspicion is that the majority of people don't practice the discipline of prayer—at least not on a regular basis. I also believe, however, that nearly everyone prays on occasion, including those who claim that they don't believe in the power of prayer. Prayer, in its most basic form, is our instinctive reaching out for God when we know that our own resources are not sufficient.

Recently I have received from friends and church members a number of testimonials about the power of prayer. Interestingly, they have not come from people who have won the lottery, hit the jackpot in a business deal, or been miraculously healed of some terrible disease. They have come from people who are suffering from disease, job loss, or lifestyle disorientation. Yet each of these individuals has testified to the power of prayer in guiding them through times of trial and crisis.

I confess to you that after forty-five years of on-the-job research on this subject, along with some very ragged and inconsistent practice of the discipline, I still haven't the foggiest notion of how or when prayer works. At times I have felt that either it doesn't work at all or I wasn't doing it correctly. Prayer remains a mystery to me, but it is a mystery I embrace and recommend.

As I grow older I believe more and more that there are no correct techniques whatsoever. Whatever you say to God, however you say it, is fully received and blessed by a God who listens better than we can speak.

So I encourage you to pray. Pray for yourself. Pray for

loved ones. Pray for your church. Pray for the world. Forget about technique and the right way to pray. Just do it. And trust that you will experience the power of God in new and refreshing ways.

7- If I Were God...

Well, I was really tempted that week. It was the same old temptation that I've had for many years. The one that got us into so much trouble back when Adam faced the same temptation. Remember? The snake said, "If you eat of this tree you will be like God" (see Genesis 3:4). That was too much temptation for Adam and his bride. And we know what happened. Nonetheless, we continue to be tempted, don't we?

It started innocently enough after the third day of rain. Most of our area had received between five and ten inches, and the ground was soaked. After thanking God profusely during the first two days, I was starting to get antsy. The abundance of run-off was causing erosion at Siete Ranch. Rain water was leaking into the north building at the church and impeding the construction on the new sanctuary. I just couldn't help it. I started thinking about the fact that, if I were God, I would do things differently.

First, I thought, if I were God I would spread this rain out more. I wasn't quarreling with the amount of rain, but just with the scheduling. For instance, what if we had gotten a couple of these inches back in July and then maybe three in August? In my head, I was working out a sprinkler schedule that makes much more sense than God's. Not only that, but I could see the results in my imagination: beautiful green pastures and lawns, and blooming flowers nearly year-round! That led to some other adjustments in temperatures and cloud cover that were calculated, I confess, to maximize my time outdoors. Inevitably, I started tinkering with the high summertime humidity levels in north Texas and . . . well, you get the idea.

I was getting pretty worked up about all of this and finally mentioned it to my own bride who, having read the story many more times than I, takes God's warning much more seriously than did Eve. Her response was pithy, to say the least: "Honey, I've told you before. Stick to sales. Stay out of management. You're no good at it."

So, to make a long story short, don't blame me if it continues to rain. And a brief reminder: It surely is true that God's long-term plans are better than our short-term thinking. I am told by experts that the tremendous soaking set up the roots of our grass and other plants in such a way that they will emerge from even a cold winter to produce a brilliant spring. I confess that, if I were God, I would not have thought about that.

7 Miracles

A friend sent me a list of purported Albert Einstein quotations. I was interested because I find Einstein to be one of the most fascinating people of the twentieth century. There were a number of quotations that I liked, but the best by far was one that has theological implications: "There are only two ways to live your life. One is as though nothing is a miracle. The other is as though everything is a miracle."

I don't know how one can walk through a pasture, view a sunrise, or watch a child at play without being struck by the wonderment of it all. The only thing that prevents us from being wide-eyed with astonishment all day long is that our senses become dull out of constant exposure to the miraculous. Think about what your reaction would be if you were to see a sunrise for the very first time.

Proof of this can be found in delivery rooms around the world. Even though the process of childbirth is well-known, it is not widely observed. Every first-time mommy and daddy exits the delivery room convinced that they have just been witness to one of the greatest of miracles.

The great French scientist, mathematician, and philosopher Blaise Pascal developed what has become known as Pascal's Wager. Essentially, he admitted that the existence of God could not be proven, but that one should wager their entire life on the possibility that God exists because there is nothing to lose. I would add to the argument by pointing out that the beauty and order we observe in the universe is difficult to explain without some concept of a Creator. How does one explain, by use of quantum mechanics or chaos theory or evolution, the existence of love, poetry, music, and self-sacrifice?

There was another quotation attributed to Einstein worth noting. Though his views of religion might have been nontraditional, he once said, "Science without religion is lame, religion without science is blind." The more he observed the universe, the more he sensed that everything is truly miraculous. May

God give us eyes to see and ears to hear so that we might embrace both the miracles of life and the mystery of creation.

7 · Words to Live By

Driving home from a meeting in May 2010, shortly after the British Petroleum oil spill in the Gulf, I listened to the radio as a correspondent interviewed a fisherman from Louisiana. It was very touching and very inspiring. This man is a crabber who doesn't know how to do his job any other way except the right way, so he culls the pregnant crabs and small crabs and returns them to the sea. The most he has ever made in one year is forty thousand dollars, but he is brought to tears by the thought of not being able to do what he loves, commenting that money could never buy him the joy that he experiences on the bayou every day.

At the end of the interview the reporter asked him for his thoughts about British Petroleum, and his answer was straightforward: "I'm sure they'll do what's right." The reporter summed up this man with a wonderful statement: "A simple faith in the honesty and humanity of others."

I couldn't help thinking that in that brief sentence we find what is missing in contemporary society. For some reason we have lost faith in the honesty and humanity of our fellow human beings. From the world of business to the world of politics, on the national stage and in our communities, we have arrived at that point where cynicism and skepticism rule the day.

Two thousand years ago an extraordinary human being

walked along the Sea of Galilee and recruited simple, honest fishermen to help him change the world forever. They preached a gospel of love and respect for all people. They urged people to just do the right thing. And they did, indeed, change the world. On that Tuesday night I heard their message echoed in the words of another fisherman who somehow maintains "a simple faith in the honesty and humanity of others."

For those who have ears to hear, these just might be words to live by.

7 The Hole in the Window

As we were getting close to the completion of the new sanctuary, a drive-by shooter aimed a gun at the stained-glass window that faces the road to the east of the church. He or she managed to shoot a high-caliber bullet through the middle pane of that window, fortunately missing workers who were on lifts inside the building. We never found the bullet and do not know if it went through the roof or lodged in a part of the mechanical system where it might eventually cause damage. We were just grateful that no one was hurt.

Unless you knew where to look you would not be able to locate the bullet hole from either inside or outside the building. Even before repairs were made, the window's spectacular beauty overshadowed the little white hole where there was no glass. Such is the nature of stained glass.

While I was trying to point out the location of the hole to our music director, it occurred to me that humans are very much like stained glass. Just as our window had a hole in the center, most of us have wounds buried deep within our hearts. We start collecting those as children when a favorite pet or a grandparent dies. We continue to accumulate them as long as we live: a lost love, a broken marriage, a child were unable to help, loved ones who die. I used to believe that once a person has grieved, everything returns to normal. I now know that sorrows are cumulative; they never completely go away. Each one leaves a little hole in the heart that most of the time cannot be detected by others.

Koinonia is a Greek word that appears in the New Testament. The word is so rich that it is difficult to fully define, but it refers to the special fellowship or community of people made possible by common experience. We experience *koinonia* in the receiving of the Eucharist, for instance, or in the sharing of a common life or purpose. *Koinonia* is fellowship made possible by the deepest bonds of the human spirit.

I truly believe that people are just like our stained glass windows: multifaceted and colorful and complex. But hidden in the center of each person is a wounded heart that cries out for love. Such is the basis for the extraordinary *koinonia* we claim as Christians. Every person is a brother or sister worthy of being embraced and loved. That means you and me, and yes, even the person who shot that bullet.

7 Neighbors

Not long ago I ordered a new shaving brush from a shop in Germany. Standard shipping was fourteen dollars, and I thought that to be reasonable since it was coming from Europe.

Immediately the company sent me an e-mail confirmation of my order and an Internet link that would allow me to track its progress. I am fascinated by this new technology, and so I tuned in to see how my package progressed.

Long story short, my shaving brush was in Germany on Wednesday, and the next morning it was delivered to my office at precisely 9:01 AM. This may not come as a surprise to those of you who regularly ship internationally, but I was stunned. I followed the flight from Germany to Memphis, then the early morning flight from Memphis to Dallas, then observed the scan at 6:00 AM. on Thursday that said it was out for delivery. Even with the advantage of the time zone changes, I would say that is pretty good service for standard shipping.

We live in an amazing world that shrinks daily. The purchase of a shaving brush can be confirmed by e-mail instantaneously, the financial transaction is immediate and seamless, and the brush can move from the hands of a German store manager to my hands in one day. This would have seemed like science fiction to not only my grandfather who died in 1960, but to my father who died in 1987.

Here is the part that I do not understand. We have a greater capacity to communicate and understand one another than ever before, so why is it that our world is torn apart by strife, hatred, and bigotry? With our ability to do business internationally and expand economic opportunity worldwide, why are there so many who are determined to pit nation against nation, culture against culture, and religion against religion? Why is it that our *ability* to communicate with and understand one another is not matched by the *will* to do so?

As I ponder this dilemma of the new flat world in which we live, I can't help but think of the Bible and the fact that life today isn't much different than it was two thousand years ago. The same strife and bigotry that you read about today can be found within the pages of the Old and New Testaments. The only thing that has changed is the technology.

When Jesus was asked "Who is my neighbor?" he didn't give the expected answer. He didn't describe what a neighbor looks like or where a neighbor lives or how a neighbor talks. He really didn't even answer the question, but instead he told a story about what it means to *be* a neighbor. This remarkable man understood a timeless secret: being neighbors has nothing to do with distance or proximity, with the ability to communicate or do business, or with technology or the lack thereof. It is about seeing in the other person—on the other side of the road or the other side of the world—a child of God who is truly a brother or sister. Until we get that part right, even FedEx isn't going to really change the world.

7 The Broken Places

There is a memorable line from Ernest Hemingway's *Farewell to Arms*: "The world breaks every one and afterward many are strong at the broken places" (Scribner, reprint edition, 2012; 216). After forty years as a pastor, I can testify to the truth of both parts of that statement.

I have said from the pulpit on many occasions that if life has not yet dealt you a severe blow, it is because you are both very lucky and very young. Sooner or later the phone call comes, the diagnosis is given, or a treasured relationship is shattered. It is part and parcel of what it means to be human, and those of us who are Christians take some comfort in the fact that even Jesus was not immune.

In 1979 the great Roman Catholic spiritualist Henri Nouwen wrote *The Wounded Healer*, a book that has been read by millions around the world. In it he unpacked the second half of Hemingway's line by suggesting that, once wounded, we always carry the scars. The broken places, however, become places of strength whereby we find opportunities to serve God by serving others. In other words, we are able to use our hurts and wounds to make a difference in the lives of other hurting humans. By doing so, we find a powerful path forward.

I have often said that we have very little power over the major events that change the trajectory of our lives. The unanticipated death of a loved one or the onset of a horrible disease enters into one's life unbeckoned and unwelcomed. What we do have control of is our interpretation of what to do with that event. When we are able, in our grief and sorrow, to start perceiving that broken place as a potential source of strength, healing begins.

This, of course, is all theoretical. I have been witness to such incredible pain in the lives of others that I marveled at how they survived (and secretly worried that I would not have). Hemingway himself came to that moment when the pain of his own life prevented him from seeing a way forward. I am convinced that, for most of us, the capacity to see the broken places as sources of strength is the action of God's grace in our lives. Powerful grace that, in Paul's words, turns weakness into strength.

I've had this Hemingway quotation sitting in a file for quite some time. I'm not exactly sure why I'm writing this right now other than the intuition that I have readers at this moment in time who need to hear a word of hope. If you are one of those, I pray that God's powerful grace will descend upon you with the good news that your brokenness will become strength, your pain will be transformed into deep joy, and your journey forward will be blessed with many opportunities to love God and serve others.

7- Generous Eyes

I was reading an online study Bible the other day and stumbled across a couple of footnotes that I thought fascinating. Since I don't read Greek, I sometimes find the footnotes to be helpful. The text was from the Gospel of Matthew (NRSV):

"The eye is the lamp of the body. So, if your eye is healthy, your whole body will be full of light; but if your eye is unhealthy, your whole body will be full of darkness. If then the light in you is darkness, how great is the darkness!" (6:22-23)

Now, here are the two footnotes: Matthew 6:22—the Greek for "healthy" here implies generous. Matthew 6:23—the Greek for "unhealthy" here implies stingy.

I know that whenever a preacher talks about generosity most people assume that he or she is revving up financial support for the church. And, of course, that is absolutely true. Well, maybe I ought to just speak for myself. I will offer a personal *mea culpa* without implicating every preacher in the universe. I am always honored and pleased to invite generous financial support for the ministries of the church because I see the number of lives that are transformed.

Having said that, this particular scripture is testimony to my ongoing theory that generosity is about much, much more than filling out a pledge card or dropping a few dollars in the plate. Generosity is about how we live life. I am fascinated by Matthew's notion of generous eyes. What do you suppose that means?

Here is what I think. Generous eyes see everything. They drink in the beauty of creation, whether it is a sunset or a newborn baby. Jesus had the most generous eyes ever, and he saw beauty in the rich young ruler (we are told that he loved him in spite of his stinginess) and in the pauper. He saw beauty in the prostitute and the leper. When he looked at someone, he saw the creation that God intended, and he spent his brief earthly life bringing healing and wholeness to the wounded parts of creation.

I do know people who tend to be stingy with their eyes. They see only what they want to see, and so they miss out on much of the beauty that God has created. Matthew tells us that if you have stingy eyes, your life will be darker than it needs to be.

If generosity is a way of life—and I think it is—it begins with the eyes. There are people who will tell us that all of this is a matter of personality, something we are born with. They will say that some people are just by nature generous and open and lively, and others are closed and stingy and withdrawn. Jesus says that's not true, that we can change who we are and how we live by opening our eyes and seeing all that God wants us to see.

My bet is on Jesus. How about you?

7 · The Light

About thirty-five years ago I gave my father-in-law the most creative and functional birthday present I've ever come up with. Bill had an old shed out in the backyard in which he had installed gas burners on which he cooked the fish that he caught. The problem was that the old shed had never been wired for electrical power. When the days were short, Bill would just pull out extension cords and trouble lights in order to see what he was doing.

One weekend when he was out of town, I wired the shed for electricity and also installed a mercury vapor light on a huge metal pole that I planted in concrete at the corner of the shed. When he got home, just in time for his birthday, he was greeted with electrical light both inside and outside of his shed.

Here is the point of this story: thirty-five years later that mercury vapor light still shines every night when the sun goes down. The shed is leaning, as is the pole, but the light is still shining. Now this part is hard to believe, but my whole family will testify to its truth: the bulb has never been changed! Neither has the electric eye that makes it come on in the dark and go off in the light. The same bulb has been shining for thirty-five years.

I have been privileged to know a few human beings like that. As Jesus commanded, they have let their light shine for decades and decades. Some of them have grown old and bent, the ravages of age apparent in their appearance, but they have never stopped being beacons of hope and love and wisdom to those who are privileged to know them.

We have a special person at our church who claims that, at age ninety-two, he suffers from TMB (too many birthdays). He wonders aloud why God has allowed him to live beyond what he considers to be a useful lifespan. Well, I think I have figured it out. It's because he is one of those beacons of light who inspire the rest of us. There is nothing useless about him if you consider the importance of the human spirit.

I know that one of these days my old mercury vapor bulb is going to emit its last ray of light, just as my friend will one day breathe his last breath. But in the meantime, they both help me to understand why Jesus used light as a metaphor in so much of his teaching and preaching. Those who shine in our midst, regardless of circumstances, are the living, breathing symbols of the powerful spiritual life that Jesus points us to. And when the time comes that they hear the words, "Well done, good and faithful servant" (Matthew 25:21 NIV), the accolade will be about much more than what they *did* in this life. It will be about who they were and what they stood for and how they inspired the rest of us.

7- The Survivors

I spent a little time one July 4 counting the dead trees at Siete Ranch. I wanted to calculate the damage of the previous year's record-breaking hot and dry summer. Much has been said and written about the number of trees that Texas would lose, but we had to wait in order to find out the truth.

Did I lose trees at Siete Ranch? Yes, about a half dozen. They were all located along a draw that flows with water whenever it rains. They were all inferior trees with shallow root systems that depend upon surface water. I did not lose a single quality tree, and the oaks that populate the northern and eastern perimeters of my place are strong and green. They have not only survived, but thrived.

I moved to Burkburnett, Texas in 1980, and it proved to be one of the hottest summers on record. The temperature often exceeded 110 degrees, and many people were worried about their trees. I was especially concerned about a majestic pecan that stood in the backyard of the parsonage, and I had considered buying one of the "root feeders" that were being peddled on TV. The concept was that you could stick this thing six feet into the ground in order to "deep water" the roots of your trees.

An old rancher told me with a grin on his face, "Son, you don't need to worry about that pecan. It has a taproot that goes farther into the ground than that tree grows above it. It won't die." And he was right.

In the fourth chapter of John, Jesus talked about a well that never goes dry. He compared the spiritual journey with the search for superficial things that never truly satisfy us. For Jesus, the choice between those two is a fundamental one that determines the quality of one's life.

How many times have we said this through the years? If you want to build a meaningful life that will weather the storms (or the droughts) that inevitably come, make the decision early to grow deep. While the world will constantly attempt to seduce you into growing the outward signs of success, only the spiritual journey will enable you to create a foundation for life that will sustain you in tough times. And make no mistake about it: tough times will come. The only question will be whether or not you are deeply rooted enough to survive and eventually thrive.

I understand why people plant inferior trees, and I have done it myself. They are cheaper and they grow faster. If you want a nice shade tree five or ten years from now, you have all sorts of inexpensive and easy options. But if you want a tree that will provide shade and comfort for your grandchildren, buy quality and be patient. The results can be seen all across Texas, both in trees and in people.

7 Reboot

Several weeks ago we had one of those technology breakdowns in one of our worship services. The microphone our worship leader was wearing suddenly stopped working. There was no warning, there was no explanation, and of course there was no apology from the technology gods. It just stopped working. And then it started again. End of story.

Back in the 1980s a friend who had helped me learn a little about computers taught me the trick of turning one off and back on again. I will always remember what he told me. He said that he was convinced that computers are like humans. They sometimes just make mistakes, and we can't explain them. When it happens, you just have to reboot them.

Does that sound like life to you? It certainly does to me. Sometimes things in my life just stop working, occasionally with no warning at all. Things will be going incredibly well and then suddenly the lawn mower won't start, the truck has a flat tire, and the wireless Internet goes on strike. Even more inexplicably, it happens in our relationships. One day you and your spouse are getting along great, and the next day there are three spontaneous arguments that seemingly rise out of no-where.

It has taken me, quite literally, decades to learn this. But most of the time these little breakdowns are not the end of the world. It doesn't mean they are fun, but it does mean that to-morrow we get to reboot and start over again.

Wisdom teaches us to keep things in perspective. In the final year of my father's life, he developed the habit of saying, "It's of no great consequence." Trust me, that saying was not consistent with the personality of the father I had known most of my life. But it was a great legacy for my brothers and me. In the big picture of life and death and deep meaning, most of the things that happen are of no great consequence.

I will finish with the quotation largely attributed to Ralph Waldo Emerson that I keep taped to my computer console, and which is a great comfort to me: "Finish each day and be done with it. You have done what you could. Some blunders and absurdities no doubt crept in; forget them as soon as you can. Tomorrow is a new day; begin it well and serenely and with too high a spirit to be cumbered with your old nonsense."

7 99.9 Percent the Same

A couple of days ago I was watching a television news show while working out early in the morning. There was a special report about what scientists have learned about DNA and the human genome. It was fascinating. Identical twins (I am one) have exactly the same DNA. Genetically speaking, they are 100 percent identical. I suspect that you knew this. But guess what? All human beings share 99.9 percent of the same DNA. Can you imagine that? Tall, short, fat, skinny, American, Asian, or Iraqi, genetically speaking we are all 99.9 percent the same!

That scientific analysis helps me understand some of the amazing things I am seeing around our church these days. For instance, an evacuee from Hurricane Katrina has become like a sister to a woman who has never at all experienced real tragedy. A mentoring family with Project Hope treats the children of their client family like their own. The youth come back from an Appa Mission Project, and they speak about some of the people they were helping as if they were long-lost aunts or uncles or grandparents. Somehow, people are being connected in extraordinary ways.

I am not blind to the divisions and hatreds that separate us. I cannot explain the terrorist who plans, and sometimes succeeds, in killing dozens or hundreds of innocent people. I have more experience with, but no better explanation for, the family members who share the same blood but who are no longer speaking to one another. But I am struck by the fact that perhaps an understanding of community or family is somehow primal, buried deep within our DNA. That it is a powerful genetic instinct that leads us to understand when one person hurts, we all hurt, and when one person is helped, all of humanity is better because of it.

I have never believed there is an inevitable conflict between science and faith. When we finally see face to face and know all there is to know, I think we will discover what our scientists are now telling us: we are all the same. That which unites us is much greater than that which divides us. That is the message of Jesus Christ. The more we live it, the more powerfully it will rule in our hearts as well as the Kingdom that God is building in our midst.

7 — Spoiled!

I spent a Monday night in my office, and not because I am a workaholic. For some reason, the electric power in our house went out, and we couldn't get anybody out to fix it. My wife opted to go to her dad's house in Frisco, but since ice was predicted for the next morning, I chose my office. My thought was that, if I get iced in, I might as well be in a place where I can get some work done.

I have to confess to you that my attitude about all of this was not exactly what one would call gracious. I was greatly irritated at the fact that staying home would mean sleeping in a cold house, even though we have the advantage of a well-insulated home, an extremely nice mattress, and dozens of blankets and comforters. When I was gathering up things to take to the office, I kept instinctively flipping light switches even though I had a flashlight in my hand. Every time I got no response, I muttered something to myself that I would not want heard in public.

It may come as no surprise to learn that an office is not an ideal place to sleep. Even though I have a couch in my office, it is more uncomfortable than the floor, so that is where I made my bed. As I was trying to fall asleep I called our director of facilities to see if he could turn off the parking lot lights because they were bothering me. (The irony of this did not occur to me until just now. I complained about no lights at the house and too much light at the office.) I managed to get a few hours of sleep and then walked to our Christian Life Center for a light workout, primarily to see if all my bones and joints were still working.

I do not think about this on a daily basis, and so I assume that you don't either. But we are all spoiled. I could have easily stayed at home. Though somewhat limited by the darkness, and perhaps uncomfortably cold when not under blankets, I would have been staying in absolute luxury compared to the childhood days of my grandparents. For instance, I had hot and cold running water because of gas water heaters, a refrigerator stashed with food that had not yet gone bad, and a cell phone to call for assistance if I needed it.

Sleeping in my office I had all of the amenities of modern life except for a mattress. I'm not sure what the number is, but millions of people go to bed every night without a mattress, including some Americans who are risking their lives to protect my freedom. As I slept, I did not have to keep a gun at my side or hear artillery shells going off nearby or worry that my village might be raided during the night.

I'm not suggesting that we all turn off the power for a night just for the experience, but I must tell you that there are spiritual rewards. The next morning, my brief prayer of gratitude included some seemingly simple things that I ordinarily take for granted. Sleeping on a concrete floor will do that for you.

7· Daily Bread

One Sunday a number of people made comments to me about how profoundly grateful they were feeling. Most acknowledged the bad news of dwindling portfolios and other assets, but they were genuine in expressing a sense of peace and hope about their lives.

Most of the comments were in response to what I said in my sermon about reciting the Lord's Prayer on a daily basis, especially this line: "Give us this day our daily bread." When Jesus first delivered that line to the disciples it was in a world where bread was the very gift of life. When people don't know where their next meal is coming from, daily bread is the most important thing for survival.

In contrast, we live in what is surely the best-fed (dare I say overfed) society in the history of civilization. Most of us only have to go to the pantry or the refrigerator in order to find many more calories than we need. If for some reason we are feeling especially hungry for something that isn't found in our kitchens, we just make a run to the local supermarket or fast-food outlet. So what does "daily bread" mean for us?

Daily bread is what God gives us in order to live fully on any particular day. It might be hope or peace or a serene spirit amidst the financial turmoil that we are experiencing. It might be the gift of courage in the face of daunting circumstances or unemployment, or the gift of faith when despair has taken a grip on one's heart. It might be the discipline to say no to alcohol or drugs. For someone who is experiencing deep depression it might be the energy just to get up and live another day. Praying the Lord's Prayer on a daily basis is our opportunity to ask God to give us whatever it is we need to sustain us through the challenges we will face that day.

The financial markets and the TV pundits and other media outlets have just about convinced us the sky is falling. But it is not. Most of us have wonderful homes to live in, kitchens and pantries fully stocked, closets that are overflowing, and the prospect of continued gainful employment. The biggest challenges we face are not about having enough money or material possessions, but about how to fully invest ourselves in the higher purposes to which God has called us.

Will you join me in asking God for daily bread this day and in the days to come? And will you join me in prayer for those who are experiencing loss?

7- "Please Touch the Flowers"

There is a sign at a silk flower vendor at Love Field Airport in Dallas that reads, "Please touch the flowers." I will never forget the first time I saw that sign several years ago and the way in which it refreshed me and put a new perspective on my day. We do, after all, spend a great deal of our time considering what we can't do, what we won't allow others to do, and what we shouldn't do. Isn't it nice sometimes to find places of affirmation that free us for celebration and joy?

I've been thinking about some of the signs we might try hanging. For instance, what about hanging a sign on your children that reads, "Please hug this child." Or maybe a sign on your co-workers that reads, "Feel free to flatter—I receive compliments well." I like the idea of a sign on the inside of our doors that reads, "You are entering the world of nature—please feel the warmth of the sun and smell the breezes in the air." Or what about a sign on all of our dining tables that reads, "Please celebrate the taste of this food and give thanks to God for the gift of nourishment." Maybe our days would all be better if we had signs hanging on our shaving or makeup mirrors that read, "Another day has been given to you. Please celebrate with joy the gift of life." What if we all had signs around our necks that read, "Gift of God: please touch and love."

There is no need to be Polyannaish. Our world is filled with a lot of bad news, and we experience that every day. But there is also a lot of good news to celebrate, a lot of love to share, a lot of flowers to touch, a lot of children to hug. It may be that part of our calling as Christians in today's world is to take some of the good news off the back pages and make headlines of what are God's gracious and tender gifts to each of us.

Chapter 9

The Seasons

Now in my seventh decade, I have become aware that the seasons of nature have become a powerful metaphor in helping me to understand the seasons of life. I relentlessly take note of the position of the sun on the horizon, the shortening or lengthening of the days and the shadows, the oscillation of the world between light and dark. What we see in the rhythm of the seasons is what we experience in profoundly personal ways in our own lives, and so the seasons teach us about ourselves.

When I was a child my favorite season was, without a doubt, summer. Long hot summers in Dallas meant no school, lots of baseball, watermelon, swimming, and homemade ice cream. I'm still partial to the seasons that have longer days and more light, but these days the moderate temperatures of late spring and early autumn provide me with the optimal conditions for doing the things I love outdoors. Nevertheless, I am learning to embrace the unique beauty and meaning of every season, and am hopeful that, by so doing, I will more fully embrace the seasons of my own life.

I hope these final reflections will help you tune in to the seasons around you and in you, and that in so doing you will experience God's grace more abundantly.

7 Shadows

I am fascinated by shadows, especially during the fall of the year. The shadows grow longer on a daily basis, foretelling shorter days and cooler weather. They signal the end of summer every bit as much as (or perhaps more than) the daily temperatures. Back in the days when I played golf regularly, I could have told you what time of the year it was by looking at the late afternoon shadows that fell across my favorite fairways.

I have been thinking about shadows and what it is that makes them act the way they do. It's odd that I have never thought about this before, but shadows don't represent reality very well. They don't grow longer because the object grows longer, nor do they disappear because the object has disappeared. They grow longer or disappear because of changes in the orientation of the object to the sun. The tree remains the same, but its shadow changes depending on the time of the day and the time of the year.

Shadows are ephemeral and untrustworthy when it comes to providing reliable information about the objects they represent. Now that I stop and think about it, Plato wrote a famous dialogue called *The Cave* in which he used an allegory about shadows to point out how difficult it is for people to accurately perceive reality.

I wonder how many of our daily life experiences are like shadows. I don't know about you, but I often get stressed over an issue that seems just huge one day, and then the next day it doesn't seem very large at all. It was just a shadow, not the real thing. By the same token I sometimes think I have found tremendous joy or a sense of great fulfillment over some temporary accomplishment or acquisition, only to discover that it was merely a shadow, not the real thing. The passing of time is what reveals the substance that lies behind the shadow.

In today's world of quick fixes and instant gratification, our Christian faith encourages us to take the long view and focus our energy on what is real and lasting rather than on that which is ephemeral and passing. It might help us to do just that if we can remember that much of what scares us or excites us in life is no more than a passing shadow.

7- Wheat

Wheat is, in some ways, a very odd plant. When the rest of the world goes dormant and everything else is yellow and dead-looking, our winter wheat here in north Texas is as green as it can be. If you drive through the country in January a hundred acres of wheat will jump out at you like a green jewel lying in the mud. And then, when spring arrives and everything else turns green, the wheat will turn golden.

It's no secret that our local wheat crops are one of the ways I measure and count the seasons. The green sprouts in the coldest and darkest part of winter are reminders that the seed is growing even when it appears that everything else is dead. And then the beauty of those "amber waves of grain" in the spring of the year is a powerful reminder of the harvest. Wheat symbolizes the good news that God is present in the rhythms of the universe and that all things have their time and place.

I encourage you to make a habit of taking a drive in the country every now and then. Take the kids or grandkids and teach them about the farmers who grow our food, and about a God who, through the miracles of nature, makes it possible. Show them the dark green wheat in the middle of winter, and return in the spring for an Easter celebration of God's wondrous work in the world.

7 Late Bloomers

It is normally early summer before you notice them. They are truly the late bloomers of the north Texas landscape. In April the earth started coming alive with color, led by the Bradford pears and other early bloomers. Then came the full litany of flowering plants, trees, and bushes opening up and serving us with remarkable beauty. All except for the crepe myrtle. It is always the lone holdout in our landscapes.

I guess the temperatures have to hit 100 degrees. We have to get to midsummer heat before these wonderful trees and bushes are willing to reveal themselves. For my taste there is no prettier plant than the crepe myrtle, and there is something special about the fact that it waits until the hottest part of the summer to bloom.

In the early 1970s, I heard Dr. Robert E. Goodrich, Jr. preach a memorable sermon titled "Bloom Where You Are Planted." As far as I know he was the first preacher to have a go with that very rich theme and, given the number of preachers who have replicated the message over the past forty years, it has certainly held up well. But often, as I sit in our backyard and observe the watermelon-colored blooms on the huge crepe myrtle in the corner of the yard, it occurs to me that there is a corollary to that theme. It is important to bloom not only *where* one is planted, but also to bloom *when* the time is right.

I have known lots of late bloomers in my life. And I have also known lots of people who shine the most when the heat is on. Winston Churchill comes to mind. Some people judge him to have been a rather mediocre and unpopular leader during times of peace, but did he ever bloom when placed in the pressure cooker of World War II! While most of the world's leaders were wilting under the heat of the Führer's blitzkrieg, Churchill set about the task of doing nothing less than saving England. One might say he was the crepe myrtle in God's garden of mid-century leaders.

Are your plans yet to unfold? Does it seem that life has dealt you a cold hand? Has love or meaning eluded you so far? It may be that you are planted in exactly the right place, but that it is not yet time to bloom. Be patient. For my money, late bloomers are some of the best.

7 Epiphany

Epiph·a·ny: **3 a** (1) : a usually sudden manifestation or perception of the essential nature or meaning of something (2) : an intuitive grasp of reality through something (as an event) usually simple and striking (3) : an illuminating discovery, realization, or disclosure (http://www.merriam-webster.com/dictionary/epiphany)

It's one of the best words in our dictionary, isn't it? It used to be limited to the vocabularies of philosophers, theologians, and poets, but these days I read it in popular books, and hear it in movies and on television. It is likely a word you have heard before, but perhaps you have not been sure of its meaning.

As a festival in the Christian church the Day of Epiphany marks the end of Christmas and the beginning of the season of Epiphany. The two Scripture verses associated with the Day of Epiphany, which always falls on January 6, are the arrival of the wise men at Bethlehem (thus revealing Jesus as a savior to the Gentiles as well as Jews) and the baptism of Jesus (revealing him as the Son of God).

The reason this word is so powerful for us is that it describes what most of us are looking for: a new insight about the meaning and purpose of life. Some of us are like the wise men and have spent money, time, and effort searching for that which can enrich our understanding of life. Others are like those standing at the edge of the crowd when Jesus was baptized: we hope for the luck of being in the right place at the right time so that we might just catch a glimpse of some eternal truth.

Either way we all are dependent on moments of epiphany because we understand that what is most important in life cannot be learned from a book, sermon, or lecture. Our most powerful moments come when God's love is unveiled for us in a sunset or the hug of a child, or in the recognition that the breath just breathed is nothing less than a silent, but divine, gift from God. These epiphanies remind us of the loving mystery that stands behind our questions that cannot be answered, our fears that cannot be conquered, and our vulnerability that cannot be overcome. They remind us that, even in the silence and the darkness, God is there.

May the days to come find you the recipient of many such moments.

7 The Dark

November is the hardest time of the year for me. The change from Daylight Saving Time and the increasing loss of evening sunlight takes its toll. Only a couple of weeks earlier, I could leave the office late in the afternoon and still have two hours or more to spend riding a horse or working around the ranch. In November it is typically dark by the time I leave the office. I have to feed the cows in the dark.

I have a rancher friend in west Texas who loves this time of the year. All of his life he has started his day at 4:30 AM and finished in late afternoon, and now he gets to spend less of his time in the dark and more in sunlight.

I have come to believe that the seasonal changes we must adapt to are good for us, even when they are painful. For one thing, they help to keep life dynamic and changing. As much as we love those perfect fall days, I feel pretty sure that our fondness for them would become less passionate if they became our daily routine for the entire year. We tend not to appreciate the things of life that can be taken for granted.

Perhaps more importantly, seasonal transitions make us stronger because they force us to adapt, physically and emotionally, to change. Those who are wise learn to find the gifts in any season of the year or any season of life. For instance, did you know that the winter sunsets in north Texas are much more spectacular than those we can view in the summer? Or that there are flowers that only bloom in the dark? If you will use the site Google to search for the term "night blooming flowers" you may be surprised to discover how much nocturnal beauty there is.

I am about to convince myself. I will never claim this is my favorite time of the year, but I am determined to find the unique gifts of the season. Like those flowers, even I can find ways to bloom in the dark. As I do so, my journey will become richer and I will discover more fully what it means to be a child of God.

7- Spring Forward

As you might guess, my rancher friend from far west Texas hates Daylight Saving Time. I understand the reason. For almost seventy years he has been getting up at 4:30 AM to go feed the cows and start his workday. In his youth that meant he worked the first hour or so in the dark, but today he feels like he spends half the day working before the sun comes up. He is not looking forward to the time change we will make to spring forward.

My take on this is much different. For me, the day we spring forward is one that I anticipate with the same kind of joy that a child experiences with the approach of Christmas. That extra hour of sunlight in the evening means I'm able to start riding horses again; it means more time outdoors, more time enjoying nature, and more time with my grandsons. It also signals the arrival of my favorite time of the year, a time when the earth turns green and is decorated by the fabulous colors of our north Texas trees and flowers. It means that the earth is emerging from winter in the same way that the butterfly emerges from the cocoon.

It occurs to me that the imagery of that last sentence is not accidental. Those of us who believe strongly in a theology of resurrection aren't totally dependent upon the biblical accounts for our faith. By my reckoning there is such abundant evidence in the life cycle of nature that the argument is difficult to refute. The seed is buried and must spend time in the darkness and cold before it begins to rise; the grass turns dormant and is covered by the snow of winter before it can be nudged into new green growth by the warming of the sun; the human heart, shrouded by the darkness of tragedy and sorrow, awakens on a warm spring morning to acknowledge that, perhaps, it will sing once again.

It is a mistake to be tempted prematurely into a full-blown proclamation of the Easter message. There are still some cold and dark days ahead of us. But the Christian journey is more joyous than arduous precisely because we carry within our very beings this profound insight. All of nature moves, inevitably, towards life rather than death, and towards the light rather than the darkness. Deep within the tomb of the cocoon the butterfly somehow knows that the best is yet to be.

7 Sunsets

One of the things I try to do every night is watch the sun go down. It is one of the best things in the world to do. It's free, and it is always different—a new show every night with no admission charge.

Each August, returning from vacation in the Davis Mountains of far west Texas, I have noticed the difference in the timing of the sunset. We in north Texas are almost six hundred miles closer to the eastern boundary of the Central Daylight Time Zone than Marfa in west Texas; Marfa is quite close to the western boundary of the time zone. Out there you get a good twenty minutes of extra daylight in the evening.

Even taking that into consideration, there is no doubt that by August the days are getting shorter. It seems like just a few days ago it was light at 9:00, and now it is perfectly dark at 8:45. When I walk out the west end of my barn alley at 8:30, the sun is setting directly in front of me. Before long it will be setting at a diagonal and everything will look different.

I can't explain why this is, but God planned the world in such a way that nothing ever sits still or stays the same. The earth is always rotating on its axis and always circling the sun, the atmosphere is always changing, and the tides are constantly on the move. This is not exactly the way most of us would have planned things. Most humans like stability and predictability, and we would have worked to get things shaped up the way we wanted and then freeze them in place.

The reason I know this is because that is what we work at all the time. We believe that if we can achieve our current set of goals, whether it is getting out of a mess or out of pain, graduating from school or getting a new job, life will be happy and predictable from that point on. That, of course, is pure illusion. We are destined for unexpected joys and unwanted pain, and sometimes unspeakable tragedy. It is the way of life.

I somehow take comfort in the rhythms of nature. If God, with such manifest wisdom and power, created the world to be in constant motion, then part of my personal spiritual journey is learning how to be comfortable with life that is dynamic rather than static, life that is not totally in my control. I don't expect I'll be fully successful at that, and I know that my questions about what appears to be the occasional irrationality of life will remain. But along the way I hope to enjoy the journey more and more. And those nightly sunsets are a big help.

7- Finding God in the Midst of the Mess

Henry Stanley Haskins once said, "What lies behind us and what lies before us are tiny matters compared to what lies within us" (*Meditations in Wall Street*; William Morrow & Company, 1940). That's a great quotation for any season of the year or any season of one's life, but I couldn't help but think how appropriate it is for the Advent and Christmas seasons.

If you are like me (and I suspect most people are), there is a tendency to be plagued by memories of the past or anxieties about the future. We want our children and grandchildren to have that perfect Christmas that will somehow conform to our recollection of some distant celebration that was without blemish. And we have wildly optimistic expectations about how this Christmas will lead us, finally, into a better New Year and an ensuing lifestyle that will encompass both prosperity and serenity.

Our obsessing about how it *used* to be or how we *want* it to be ends up being the Grinch that stole Christmas. Being so focused on the past or the future prevents us from being centered in the present, which is, by the way, the only place where serenity can be found. It is also found only in the world that lies within us, not in outward circumstances.

There is no better illustration of this than the nativity itself, that quintessential symbol, for most of us, of true peacefulness. God knew what he was doing when he placed the Holy Family in the midst of cold and filthy conditions, leaving us with no other conclusion than that true serenity is a matter of the heart rather than the size of the mansion or the current status of the consumer confidence index.

So here's my encouraging word: Embrace the imperfections that surround this season in the same way that Joseph and Mary embraced the stable. You may not find the perfect present, the party probably won't go off without a hitch, and the family gathering may blow up once again. It's okay. God comes to be born within us. God is the serenity that is found in the midst of the mess.

7- The Snowman

Here we are, seven days out from the historic snowfall of last week. Today the sun is shining brightly, and temperatures are supposed to reach nearly sixty degrees. For the most part it looks like we are edging toward spring. And yet, as I drive around town, I still see occasional balls of snow sitting out in a yard or field. At first I didn't understand how that could be, but I finally figured it out: they were the last remains of someone's snowman!

Right before Christmas I watched a cartoon movie with my grandson about how an evil entrepreneur invented a substance that would instantly melt all the snow and ice that causes so much winter trouble in northern areas. You could just go around spraying this stuff, and it would all disappear. Most of the adults liked the idea, but the children hated it. Not only that, Frosty the Snowman was scared to death that he would meet his demise. In the end, the evil spray was destroyed, and everyone was happy.

Time marches on relentlessly, and it always does some damage. It eventually melts the greatest snowman ever built; it deteriorates the homes we grew up in; it changes the culture we once understood and felt comfortable in. I am learning that its relentless attack on aging bodies can be resisted, but not defeated, and I sometimes feel like that snowman that is just slowly melting away.

But in the final analysis time is our friend and not our enemy. It replaces the melting ball of snow with flowers and green grass; it challenges us to grow by changing; and it ultimately replaces the aging body with a spirit that is fully attuned to the kingdom of God.

7 Hope

I often struggle during the months of January and February as we experience the final days of winter. I am a warm weather person, and I sometimes become so eager for spring that it is painful. I yearn for those days when the ground warms, the grass and trees begin to turn green, the earth comes to life once again. The last couple of weeks have been especially tough as we have experienced lots of rain along with some sleet and ice.

About this time every year I think of the great French novelist Albert Camus who, along with philosopher Jean-Paul Sartre, led the French existentialist movement during the middle of the twentieth century. The existentialists were known for their dark, cynical view of life. And yet Camus could not escape the heartbeat of hope that God had planted within him. He wrote what is perhaps the most memorable line in existentialist literature: "In the depth of winter, I finally learned that within me there lay an invincible summer" (Albert Camus, "Return to Tipasa," *Lyrical and Critical Essays* [New York: Alfred A. Knopf, 1970], 169).

That quotation is almost biblical in its profound truth. Will spring ever get here? You bet. It is as inevitable as the rising of the sun. And if you are personally going through a winter of despair or illness or trouble, the same is true. It may seem as if the dark, cold days of your life will never end, but they will. God has planted within you the seeds of hope, and that hope is not in vain. Spring is on the way and with it the great day of Resurrection that we call Easter. So it is in your life as well. Celebrate the good news of what God is doing in your life even in the darkest of days.

7 Let Him Easter in Us

The great Victorian poet Gerard Manley Hopkins once brilliantly used the word Easter as a verb: "Let him easter in us, be a dayspring to the dimness of us...." I love that phrase because it clearly implies that Easter is not just a celebration that we attend one day out of the year, but is God living in us and changing us from the inside out. It is not just about what we say, but about what we do.

I once read a sermon that posed the question of what might be different if you were to allow Easter to be a verb in your life. If Easter were a verb, how would it change your relationships? What might a resurrected relationship look like? If Easter were a verb, how would it transform your sense of commitment to those who have not been granted the rich opportunities many of us enjoy?

If Easter were a verb, how might it change the way in which you look at the future? If the Resurrection has guaranteed us God's victory of life over death, forgiveness over sin, hope over despair, what would it mean to live expectantly and joyously and fully in that reality?

As for me, it is easier said than done. Still I pray, "Dear God, come and Easter in me."

7 Stuck!

One Monday night I drove to Siete Ranch to feed the cows. As I turned onto FM 902 to cross the railroad tracks, I noticed that the flashing barriers were down because of an oncoming train. I put my truck in park and turned off the engine to wait it out. It was then that I noticed what was happening.

A little red car that had been coming from the other direction was stuck on the railroad track, caught between the flashing barriers. I don't know how it happened, but it could not move because it was blocked not only by the barriers, but also by cars both behind and in front of the barriers. The approaching train was still far down the track, but its arrival was inevitable.

As I sat there and watched this predicament, it occurred to me that this is how some people surely feel about life. There are those who feel like they are stuck in life, and all they can see is the inevitable marching of time, grim mortality rushing toward them. I confess there are moments when I feel that way myself. As we all know, life speeds up as one ages, and sometimes the end appears to be approaching faster than is comfortable.

I couldn't help thinking about Easter. At its most basic, Easter is the proclamation of the Church that there is more than meets the eye: more than mere existence, more than waiting for mortality to catch up with us, more than a timeline of opportunity punctuated by meaningless death. The Easter message is what keeps us from getting stuck between the surprising joy of birth and the inevitability of death.

What happened to the little red car? The cars in front managed to move back enough to allow the little red one to maneuver between and out of the barriers. Disaster averted.

Ironically, the story of the Resurrection is not as unambiguous. It is a story still shrouded in mystery, the Gospel writers offering various accounts of the post-Resurrection appearances and the responses to them. We are left somewhat in suspense, the story not yet fully finished. But this much we do know: Hope defeated Despair; Life defeated Death; Love defeated Hate. On the other side of the Cross the disciples became passionate witnesses to the love of Christ, and they changed the course of history.